NO BORDERS, NO LIMITS
NIKKATSU ACTION CINEMA

This second edition published by FAB Press Ltd, July 2008
(The first edition was published by FAB Press, October 2007)
FAB Press Ltd, 2 Farleigh, Ramsden Road, Godalming, GU7 1QE, England, U.K.
www.fabpress.com

Acknowledgements
This book began as a catalogue for a retrospective of Nikkatsu Action films at the Udine Far East Festival in Udine, Italy in April 2005. The enthusiasm and support of Yasue Nobusawa of Nikkatsu and Sabrina Baracetti and Thomas Bertacche of the Udine festival made both the catalogue and the retro a reality. Also of great assistance were Mamiko Kawamoto, who was the Japan coordinator for the Udine festival, and Richard Harvis, who edited the Nikkatsu Action retro catalogue.
I would also like to thank Outcast Cinema's Marc Walkow, who has done more work than anyone else to promote interest in Nikkatsu Action movies in North America since the publication of this book's first edition.

For this FAB Press edition I owe much to Tom Mes and Francis Brewster, who proofed the text and provided many valuable suggestions, and FAB Press publisher Harvey Fenton, who overcame many hurdles to make this project a reality. I would also like to thank Shinako Matsuda and Hideo Iwamoto of Nikkatsu for their cooperation and assistance.

The posters and stills for the book are used with the permission of Nikkatsu and are copyright © Nikkatsu Corporation. The photos of Keiichiro Akagi, Ruriko Asaoka, Yujiro Ishihara, Akira Kobayashi, Hideaki Nitani, Joe Shishido and Koji Wada are sourced from "Heibon" and "Shukan Heibon" magazines. Joe Shishido's agency, I&M, also supplied photos, as did Seijun Suzuki's agency, Ogura Jimusho. The photo of Toshio Masuda was taken by the author.

This book is dedicated to Joe-san and Masuda Kantoku, for making it all come to life.

Front cover illustration
Jerry Fujio *(left)* and Joe Shishido *(right)* take aim in "A Colt Is My Passport" (Colt wa Ore no Passport, 1967).
Back cover illustration
Original theatrical poster for "Gangster VIP" (Burai Yori Daikanbu, 1968).
Frontispiece illustration
Original theatrical poster for "Red Glass" (Akai Gurasu, 1966).
Title page illustration
Nikkatsu Corporation logo.

NO BORDERS NO LIMITS

Nikkatsu Action Cinema

日活株式会社

Mark Schilling

Contents

No Borders, No Limits

Foreword

The label said it all: Nikkatsu *Akushon*. Nikkatsu was a studio that had been around since the silent days and Akushon was "action," written in the katakana syllabary for foreign words. During their peak, from the late 1950s to the early 1960s, Nikkatsu Action films evoked a cinematic world neither foreign nor Japanese, but a mix of the two, where Japanese tough guys had the swagger, moves and even long legs of Hollywood movie heroes. Where the Tokyo streets, Yokohama docks and Hokkaido plains took on an exciting, exotic aura, as though they were stand-ins for Manhattan, Marseilles or the American West.

To young audiences growing to adulthood in post-war Japan, that mix was not just fantasy: it reflected the Western influences all around them, from cowboy movies to bop jazz, from the big American cars on the city streets to the cavernous nightclubs where hip urbanites could drink bourbon, dance the mambo and rub shoulders with real-life tough guys – the yakuza.

At the same time, Nikkatsu Action was less gritty realism than macho romanticism, where one guy with guts, smarts and quick fists could win the day over a whole gang of hoods, in an internationalised space outside the usual Japanese matrix of family, community and workplace, with its myriad of obligations and rules.

One young Nikkatsu Action fan, Takenobu Watanabe, later published a collection of essays on the genre titled *The Beautiful World of Nikkatsu Action* (*Nikkatsu Akushon no Kirei na Sekai*). He found that beauty in the genre's borderless, cosmopolitan style and stance.

The Nikkatsu Action world was not that of Yasujiro Ozu or Kenji Mizoguchi, directors with emotional roots in pre-war Japan, who affirmed their Japanese identity in their post-war films. It was not even the world of Nagisa Oshima, Masahiro Shinoda or Shohei Imamura, the leaders of the Japanese Nouvelle Vague, who distrusted authority, cinematic or otherwise, while viewing post-war society as a jungle where traditional values were devalued and the amorally strong flourished.

Their looks through the social glass darkly were not what the big audience wanted, their studio bosses complained, with some justification (though several Nouvelle Vague films became box office hits). What it wanted, Nikkatsu discovered, beginning in 1956 with Takumi Furukawa's *Season of the Sun* (*Taiyo no Kisetsu)*, was sun, surf, youthful rebellion – and Yujiro Ishihara, a lanky, long-legged kid who radiated punkish charm, and could punch his way out of trouble with almost contemptuous ease. Foreigners may have admired Toshiro Mifune's sweaty intensity as quintessentially Japanese, but Japanese youth preferred Yujiro's brand of casual, Westernised cool.

He presented an opportunity – and a dilemma – to Nikkatsu executives. They had the hottest star in Japan, but the so-called "Sun Tribe" (*Taiyozoku*) phenomenon he represented, of privileged kids indulging appetites for kicks and sex with little regard for conventional morality, was not only roundly condemned by the guardians of said morality, but had no future. When the fad was over, would Yujiro's career be history as well?

Faced with a similar dilemma in Elvis Presley, Hollywood paired him with reliable hack directors (Michael Curtiz, Norman Taurog, Richard Thorpe), who ground out a series of formula films targeted strictly at fans. Instead of nurturing his career, the studios enclosed it in a strange, air-tight bubble called the Elvis Movie.

Nikkatsu took a different approach because it saw, in a way that Hollywood did not, what was going on outside the studio walls. Sun Tribesmen swimming, sailing and hanging out on the Shonan Coast near Tokyo may have been relatively few in number, but their less privileged contemporaries were fascinated by what they represented: more freedom (and licence) for the individual than was possible in tradition-bound, group-oriented Japan.

Yujiro epitomised that new individualism – a kid who said what he thought and did what he wanted, as though it were the most natural thing in the world. No agonizing over violating codes or offending seniors. Instead he laughed at his enemies and, if he was pushed, pushed back. He didn't have a single cringe in his body – or soul. As an actor, he was willing to try anything, as long as he could be himself.

So Nikkatsu tried him in every known genre, from musicals to melodramas, but discovered that he had a talent for action. The studio also felt its young directors could better connect with Yujiro's young fans. So, starting in 1957, Yujiro made more action films with newcomers like Toshio Masuda and Koreyoshi Kurahara, only several years his elder. It was as if Elvis had worked with Richard Lester (born in 1932) instead of Michael Curtiz (born in 1886). These films and others like them were hits and a spawned a new genre: Nikkatsu Action.

Though set in contemporary Japan, Nikkatsu Action films reflected mostly a thin, urban slice of its reality. Yokohama and the Ginza made frequent appearances, while anonymous suburban bedtowns and dull provincial cities made few. The sounds heard off screen were fog horns or boat whistles, not the more common cries of sweet potato or laundry pole sellers.

Characters were forever ordering whiskies at fancy nightclubs, while flamenco dancers stomped or foreign couples swung and swayed. They rarely went into raucous *izakaya* (Japanese-style pubs) to drink sake, while drunks wailed their favourite *enka* (Japanese ballads). They were often police detectives or pilots or boxers; seldom salarymen. They pursued their enemies in speed boats or new-model cars (both then far beyond the reach of the average punter), not on bicycles or trains.

This selective, glamorised view of national life was the strategy of Hollywood, but Nikkatsu Action directors also took their cues from Duvivier, Fellini, Godard and other European models, just as their young fans were listening to chanson and canzone, as well as jazz and rock'n'roll.

This style – in Japan but not of it – was carried to an extreme in the Eastern Westerns of another young Nikkatsu star, Akira Kobayashi. The Japanese back country of his nine *Wanderer* (*Wataridori*, 1959-1962) series films resembled, in its wilder reaches, the mountains and plains of the Old West, if not its deserts. But his character, a drifter who clip-clopped along mountain roads on a horse, with bullwhip and guitar, was a pure invention, as were his adventures on ranches or in mining towns that looked as though they had been imported lock, stock and hitching post from Colorado.

Still, for young audiences raised on the Hollywood romance of the Old West, on the big screen or small, the *Wanderer* films were at least possible dreams. Perhaps the real parallels were, not celluloid Westerns about a vanished age, but the present-day TV exploits of Roy Rogers, who gave American Baby Boomers hope that the Western adventure might still live, even if the cowboys drove jeeps.

In making these and other so-called "borderless action" (*mukokuseki akushon*) films, Nikkatsu directors and stars may have borrowed heavily from foreign models, but the results were less copies than reinventions – like a Japanese pizzeria that uses an "authentic" Sicilian crust, but tops it with squid and mayonnaise. Joe Shishido, the most comically outrageous "un-Japanese" (*Nihonjin banare*) of Nikkatsu's stable of stars, may have learned to twirl a pistol by watching Kirk Douglas in *Man Without a Star*, but his leering, grinning, motor-mouth bad guy persona was strictly his own.

In the mid-1960s, as its stars, directors and audiences aged, Nikkatsu Action films began to take on a darker, more adult tone. Ishihara was no longer a carefree youth on screen, but a conflicted man with a past. His films from this period were called "mood action" (*mudo akushon*) – and the mood was usually down. Instead of dancing the night away with frequent co-star Ruriko Asaoka, he was often alone at the bar, nursing a drink – and remembering.

By this time, the entire Japanese film industry was in a funk, with its audiences at home, glued to the tube, while theatres all over the country were closing their doors. The Nikkatsu Action dream was dying – or rather becoming middle-aged.

New stars, including Tetsuya Watari, Tatsuya Fuji and Meiko Kaji, revived it in the mid-to-late-1960s, while directors like Seijun Suzuki and Yasuharu Hasebe brought a new, unfettered sensibility. Too unfettered in the case of Suzuki, who was fired by the studio after the 1967 release of *Branded to Kill* (*Koroshi no Rakuin*).

The Nikkatsu films of this period still looked Westward – Hasebe's 1966 debut *Black Tight Killers* (*Ore ni Sawaru to Abunai ze*) had the look of a James Bond spoof,

Akira Kobayashi has more than a gold-plated beauty on his mind in Yasuharu Hasebe's Nikkatsu New Action classic "Black Tight Killers" (Ore ni Sawaru to Abunai ze, 1966).

日K活 俺にさわると危ないぜ 映倫 *25*

though the hero, played by Kobayashi, was a photographer just back from Vietnam, not a spy. At the same time, many of them reflected an industry trend toward home-grown forms, such as the popular yakuza movies, set in the pre-war period, whose heroes upheld the traditional *giri-ninjo* code of selfless loyalty to elders and consideration for underlings – and made their cool moves with swords instead of pistols.

From 1968 to 1971 yet another sub-genre, "New Action" (*Nyu Akushon*), arose that resisted this trend – upholding individualism, even if it meant making the hero dirty and his world chaotic and violent. But so were the city streets and campuses where activists fought pitched battles with riot police. And so were the highways where biker gangs roared through the night, horns blasting sleeping citizens into wide-eyed fury.

New Action films about the latter types often had plenty of energy, but compared with the Sun Tribe films of a decade and a half earlier, the vibe was angrier, harsher and stranger. It was like the contrast between The Stooges and early Elvis. But just as Iggy Pop sold fewer records than Elvis, New Action stars drew far fewer fans than Ishihara at his peak. Nikkatsu's box office shrank – until the end came in 1971.

Foreign critics long ignored Nikkatsu Action. Donald Richie and Joseph Anderson's seminal 1959 history *The Japanese Film: Art and Industry* passed over the entire genre in silence, as did its 1982 revised edition. Joan Mellen's 1976 study *The Waves at Genji's Door: Japan Through Its Cinema* does not mention Nikkatsu or its films and stars even once. The rise of Seijun Suzuki to cult fame in the West in the 1980s brought the genre more attention abroad, but often in a negative way, with critics hailing Suzuki as an overlooked and discarded master, while dismissing the films of his colleagues as studio hack work (despite having seen few of them).

For the 2005 edition of the Udine Far East Film Festival I programmed a retrospective of sixteen Nikkatsu Action films, minus any by Suzuki. My aim was not to challenge the critical consensus – Suzuki is a master, after all – but to broaden the discussion. Given that Suzuki's Nikkatsu films had been widely screened and distributed abroad for two decades, I did not feel that, given the festival's limited program slots, we needed to screen masterpieces like *Branded to Kill* (*Koroshi no Rakuin*, 1967) and *Gate of Flesh* (*Nikutai no Mon*, 1964) yet again, even though they were among the best work of our guest, Joe Shishido.

Instead, we presented a representative non-Suzuki selection from all periods of Nikkatsu Action, featuring top stars, including Yujiro Ishihara, Akira Kobayashi, Keiichiro Akagi, Joe Shishido and Tetsuya Watari, and directors, including Koreyoshi Kurahara, Yasuharu Hasebe and Toshio Masuda, who also attended as a guest. The films were:

Black Tight Killers (Ore ni Sawaru to Abunai ze, 1966)
A Colt Is My Passport (Colt wa Ore no Passport, 1967)
Crimson Pistol (Kurenai no Kenju, 1961)
Dirty Work (Rokudenashi Kagyo, 1961)
Fast-Draw Guy (Hayauchi Yaro, 1961)
Gangster VIP (Burai Yori Daikanbu, 1968)
Glass Johnny: Look Like a Beast (Glass Johnny: Yaju no yo ni Miete, 1962)
Plains Wanderer (Daisogen no Wataridori, 1962)
Red Handkerchief (Akai Handkerchief, 1964)
Red Quay (Akai Hatoba, 1958)
Roughneck (Arakure, 1969)
Rusty Knife (Sabita Knife, 1958)
Season of Heat (aka *Warped Ones*) *(Kyonetsu no Kisetsu*, 1960)
Stray Cat Rock: Sex Hunter (Nora Neko Rock: Sex Hunter, 1970)
Tales of a Gunman: Quick-Draw Ryu (Kenju no Buraicho: Nukiuchi no Ryu, 1960)
Velvet Hustler (Kurenai no Nagareboshi, 1967)

This book was originally published to accompany the Udine retro – thus the emphasis on the above films, directors and stars, including interviews with Shishido and Masuda. For this FAB Press edition, I have rewritten the article on Seijun Suzuki to more clearly reflect his importance, not in the Nikkatsu studio system – where his work was undervalued – but world cinema, where he has earned his rightful place as a true original, whose films continue to baffle, astonish and delight.

I have also added profiles of actors who made major contributions to the Nikkatsu Action genre, including its Nikkatsu New Action spin-off, but were not included, for reasons of space and priority, in the Udine festival book.

There are dozens more Nikkatsu Action actors and directors to be profiled, hundreds more films to be critiqued and much more to be written about the studio's history, at least in English. This is an introduction to a genre that not only produced enduring films, but also had a major impact on the popular culture in post-war Japan.

For the convenience of general readers, I have used Western name order throughout the book. I have also rendered words originally written in the katakana syllabary in Roman letters. Thus Nikkatsu *Akushon* becomes Nikkatsu Action.

I have also discussed the plots of certain films in several places in the text, if not in precisely the same words. This repetition exists for the convenience of the majority of readers, who will dip into the book at parts that interest them – and will want a description of what a given film is about then and there, rather than thumb back to its first mention. For those who read the book straight through – and become annoyed at being told, for the third time, what *Crazed Fruit* is about, I apologise.

Keiichiro Akagi, one of Nikkatsu's "Diamond Line" of top male stars.

The History of Nikkatsu

Japan's oldest motion picture studio, Nikkatsu was founded in 1912 by four companies that intended to monopolise film production and distribution in Japan on the model of the Motion Picture Patents Company – the trust that was the bane of early Hollywood. Originally called *Nippon Katsudo Shashin* (Japan Cinematograph Company), the company later shortened its name to Nikkatsu.

With Japan's first true director, Shozo Makino, and star, Matsunosuke Onoe, on the payroll, Nikkatsu was an industry power from the start, though its trust plans never bore fruit. In the 1910s, its Kyoto studio produced period dramas, while its new studio in Mukojima, Tokyo specialised in films based on *Shinpa* – a theatrical form that used contemporary settings and situations, but with a Kabuki-influenced performance style.

In the 1920s, under pressure from Shochiku and other forward-looking rivals, Nikkatsu incorporated new filmmaking methods imported from the West while switching from *oyama* – men playing women's roles in accordance with Kabuki convention – to actresses.

One of its most progressive talents in this period was Kenji Mizoguchi, who had made his directing debut in 1923, at the age of twenty-four. Instead of *Shinpa* dramas, Mizoguchi filmed stories about modern Japanese, particularly the lower and middle classes – a lead that other Nikkatsu directors would follow. Initially on the melodramatic side, his depictions of contemporary life took a more realistic, socially critical turn later in the decade, part of a wider movement toward making so-called "tendency films" (*keiko eiga*) influenced by leftist thought.

In 1929, Nikkatsu released two features made using a primitive sound-on-disc system, but their failure at the box office delayed the studio's switch to sound. In 1932 it experimented again, this time more successfully, with Mizoguchi's *Timely Mediator* (*Toki no Ujigama*), and, after joining forces with Western Electric in 1933, began importing the most advanced Hollywood sound equipment.

The studio's management, however, alienated the hired help with its stingy payments, high-handed attitudes and old-fashioned production methods. Its top stars and directors, including Mizoguchi, Tomu Uchida, Daisuke Ito, Tomotaka Tasaka and Minoru Murata, left the studio in droves in the early years of the decade.

In 1933 there was a shake-up at the top, with Sadatomo Nakatani taking over as president from studio founder Einosuke Yokota. Nakatani's new management team included Kanichi Negishi as head of production and Kyusaku Hori as managing director. Negishi was able to lure back a few of the defectors, including Uchida and Tasaka, while Hori got himself in legal trouble over alleged bribes and stock manipulation – and ended up in jail.

That same year Nikkatsu acquired a studio in the Tamagawa district of Tokyo from a failed rival and, following renovations, used it to make its contemporary films. Meanwhile, at Nikkatsu's Kyoto studio, talented young directors like Sadao Yamanaka and Hiroshi Inagaki were churning out swashbuckling samurai pictures called *chanbara eiga*. Their top stars, including Chiezo Kataoka and Denjiro Okochi, had a huge popular following.

As the war on the continent intensified and censorship tightened, Nikkatsu, in common with other Japanese studios, began making so-called "national policy" (*kokusaku*) propaganda films. In 1941, the government asked the ten leading film companies, including Nikkatsu, to re-organise into two. A counterproposal for three companies was accepted and in 1942 Nikkatsu, at Hori's suggestion, merged its production facilities with those of the Shinko and Daito studios in a new entity, while retaining a separate identity as a theatre management company.

The new merged studio, called Daiei, survived the war, though it was weakened by its lack of a theatre network. Meanwhile, Nikkatsu returned to prosperity in the early post-war period by screening Hollywood films in its theatres. Starved for entertainment and wowed by Hollywood glamour and production values, Japanese audiences crowded in, doubling the box office for foreign films between 1951 and 1953. After a long spell of labour troubles and struggles with Occupation-era censorship, the Japanese film industry also grew rapidly in the early 1950s – and Hori, now the studio head, decided in 1953 that the time was ripe to re-enter production.

Flush with cash from its prosperous exhibition business, Nikkatsu built new offices in downtown Tokyo and a new studio complex near its pre-war Tamagawa studio, now owned by Daiei. The five major studios – Toho, Shochiku, Daiei, Toei and Shin Toho – joined forces to block this Nikkatsu move, both to prevent the dilution of their profits and the defection of their talent to the Nikkatsu banner.

But Nikkatsu, with its fat chequebook, modern facilities and promises of wider opportunities, was able to recruit the personnel it needed to restart production in 1954, after a twelve-year hiatus. With producer Wahei Hoshino in charge, and the veteran Tasaka and promising new directors like Kon Ichikawa and So Yamamura under contract, Nikkatsu began making films, though of the eleven released in 1954, only Yamamura's *Black Current* (*Kuroi Ushio*) was a hit.

That same year Shochiku producer Takeshi Yamamoto cast his lot with Nikkatsu, bringing along assistant directors Ko Nakahira, Buichi Saito, Katsumi Nishikawa and Kiyoshi Horiike, as well as director Yuzo Kawashima, actor Tatsuya Mihashi and actresses Mie Kitahara, Yumeji Tsukioka and Izumi Ashikawa – several of whom would later play key roles in Nikkatsu's success.

The Big Five opposed Nikkatsu's production of *The Moon Doesn't Rise* (*Tsuki wa Noborinu*) – the second film directed by pre-war superstar Kinuyo Tanaka.

Undeterred, Tanaka made and released the film in January 1955, using a script co-written by Yasujiro Ozu. She was not, however, able to cast her first choices, including Keiko Kishi, Keiji Sada and Yoshiko Kuga, then all under contract to Shochiku. Enraged by this interference, Ozu threatened to quit Shochiku, where he had spent his entire career, and go freelance. The press whooped up this controversy, but the Big Five couldn't stop the Nikkatsu production line.

In 1955 it moved into full gear, with one film a week rolling into theatres. Nikkatsu product in this period was a mix of genres, including period dramas (Masahiro Makino's *Tales of Jirocho: The Akiba Festival* [*Jirochogaiden Akiba no Himatsuri*]), literary adaptations (Kon Ichikawa's *The Heart* [*Natsume Soseki no Kokoro*]) and comedies (Yuzo Kawashima's *Baggage of Love* [*Ai no Nimotsu*]) – though the overall flavour was more Western than Japanese.

The film that became the studio's first mega-hit and launched its first real star was Takumi Furukawa's *Season of the Sun* (*Taiyo no Kisetsu*), released in May 1956. Based on a prize-winning novel by Shintaro Ishihara, *Season of the Sun* was a drama of contemporary youth starring Hiroyuki Nagato as an amoral high school boy and Yoko Minamida as a girl he meets in the Ginza, seduces and, when she starts to become serious, abandons.

The film was considered controversial for its treatment of adolescent sex, pregnancy and abortion, against a backdrop of wild living (as then conceived) on the Shonan Coast, but for much of the audience, particularly the female portion of it, a main attraction was Yujiro Ishihara, Shintaro's younger brother, who played the hero's boxing club friend. With his long legs – then a rare sight in Japanese films – and combination of punkish insolence and boyish charm, Yujiro embodied new winds of freedom blowing through the land.

The film became a big hit and the Shonan Coast, southwest of Tokyo, became Japan's Malibu and Riviera, a place where young fashionables, called the Sun Tribe, summered in imitation of the film's heroes.

Yujiro's true launching pad to stardom, however, was *Crazed Fruit* (*Kurutta Kajitsu*, 1956). Once again, Shintaro wrote the novel on which the film was based, while first-time director Ko Nakahira injected a fresh, bold sensibility into his tale of passion, betrayal and death, set among the upper middle class on the Shonan Coast. The film, about two teenage brothers (Ishihara and Masahiko Tsugawa) who both fall for the same seemingly pure-hearted girl (Mie Kitahara), became a box office sensation in Japan and was praised by François Truffaut, then about to make his own mark as a leader of the French New Wave.

With Ishihara now a national idol – the living embodiment of the Sun Tribe ethos – Nikkatsu began casting him in film after film. The Sun Tribe boom proved brief, though. Outraged guardians of public morals, including industry censors, protested the depictions of youthful licence, however true to life, and Nikkatsu, bowing to pressure, halted production of a film based on yet another Shintaro novel, *The Gray Classroom* (*Haiiro no Kyoshitsu*).

Ishihara, however, was unstoppable, appearing in, quick succession in the family drama *The Baby Carriage* (*Ubaguruma*), the war drama *Human Torpedo Attack* (*Ningengyorai Shutsugekisu*), the musical *The Birth of the Jazz Girls* (*Jazz Musume Tanjo*), the literary adaptation *Lunar Eclipse* (*Gesshoku*) and the period comedy *The Sun's Legend* (*Bakumatsu Taiyoden*). In 1957 he began starring in the action films that were to define the next stage of his career, as well as Nikkatsu's image for the next decade and a half, including Umetsugu Inoue's *The Winner* (*Shorisha*), *The Eagle and the Hawk* (*Washi to Taka*) and *The Guy Who Started a Storm* (*Arashi o Yobu Otoko*), as well as Koreyoshi Kurahara's debut feature, *I Am Waiting* (*Ore wa Matteiru ze*). Featuring Ishihara as a punkish drummer who battles his way to the top in the Ginza jazz scene, *The Guy Who Started a Storm* was a mega-hit that established Ishihara's stardom and saved Nikkatsu's fortunes.

In 1958 film attendance in Japan reached an all-time peak – 1.1 billion – and Ishihara was the star fans most wanted to see. He continued to work mainly in the action genre, including Toshio Masuda's *Rusty Knife* (*Sabita Knife*) and *Red Quay* (*Akai Hatoba*). The latter, a reworking of *Pépé le Moko*, set the pattern for the "borderless" (*mukokuseki*) action films that would become a Nikkatsu mainstay.

Realising that Ishihara's action hits were more than a flash in the pan, Nikkatsu made more films in that genre in 1959. The studio's big New Year's film was Umetsugu Inoue's *The Friendship That Started a Storm* (*Arashi o Yobu Yujo*), featuring rising star Akira Kobayashi in a story that, like that of *The Guy Who Started a Storm*, was set in Tokyo's jazz world. Soon after, Toshio Masuda released *Forget About Women* (*Onna o Wasurero*), starring Kobayashi as a boxer who finds a new life and love after blinding an opponent in the ring. The film was a success commercially and critically, giving Kobayashi another push toward stardom.

He soon scored another, bigger hit with Buichi Saito's *Leaving Tosa of the South* (*Nangoku Tosa o Ato ni Shite*), playing an ex-con who returns home to Kochi and tries to build a straight life with an old flame, but is pulled back into the gang life by the dirty deeds of a rival.

Akira Kobayashi completed his miracle year with headlining appearances in Hiroshi Noguchi's *Ginza 'Mite Guy* (*Ginza Maitogai*) and Saito's *Guitar Wanderer* (*Guitar o Motta Wataridori*). The former film, the first in a six-part series, depicted the adventures of a Ginza man-about-town ("'Mite," the first part of Kobayashi's nickname, was a contraction of "dynamite"), while in the later, a first of a nine-part series, Kobayashi played a drifter who breaks up a smuggling ring in the northern port of Hakodate, then sails off into the sunset. The *Wanderer* films were modelled

above: Hideaki Nitani.
opposite: The "Diamond Line". *(from left):* Keiichiro Akagi, Koji Wada, Akira Kobayashi, Yujiro Ishihara.

on Hollywood Westerns, right down to Akira's guitar, boots, fringes and horse. They also made a star of Ruriko Asaoka, who played his love interest in the first eight instalments.

In 1959 Koji Wada, a teenager scouted for his resemblance to Ishihara, debuted in Katsumi Nishikawa's *Silent Struggle* (*Mugen no Ranto*), while Keiichiro Akagi, a hunky college dropout, starred in Seijun Suzuki's *The Naked Age* (*Suppadaka no Nenrei*). Both actors proved popular with fans and joined Ishihara and Kobayashi in what Nikkatsu began calling, in February 1960, its "Diamond Line" of top male stars. Nikkatsu cranked out action films with this quartet much the way a baseball manager rotates his starting pitchers.

That year Akagi, or "Tony" as he was nicknamed for his perceived resemblance to Tony Curtis, also appeared in Hiroshi Nomura's *Tales of a Gunman: Quick-Draw Ryu* (*Kenju Buraicho: Nukiuchi no Ryu*), the first of a four-part series about a hitman who nicks, but never kills, his targets. Another rising talent, Joe Shishido, played Akagi's wise-cracking rival.

Meanwhile, Wada starred in *The Flying Kid* (*Sottobi Kozo*), a hit film that was a comic, teen-targeted take-off on the *Wataridori* films and the first entry in his *Kozo* (*Kid*) series. He also made seven films with Seijun Suzuki, starting with *Fighting Delinquents* (*Kutabare Gurentai*, 1960), a comic actioner that was Suzuki's first colour film. Wada's time as Nikkatsu's teen sensation was to be short, however. Though part of the Diamond Line, he was really more of an idol than a full-fledged action star – and idol fans, then as now, soon moved on to the next pretty face. Wada, however, remained a Nikkatsu regular throughout the 1960s.

Not to be outdone by the newcomers, Kobayashi starred in *The Drifter Who Came from the Sea* (*Umi Kara Kita Nagaremono*, 1960), the first of his five-part *Drifter* (*Nagaremono*) series. Directed by Tokujiro Yamazaki, these films featured Kobayashi as a drifter who comes to town, battles various bad guys and becomes involved with a local girl, but leaves her in the last reel. Once again, Ruriko Asaoka played the girl, Joe Shishido, the comic rival who turned ally by the end.

With all four of its stars raking in yen, the Diamond Line seemed likely to roll on indefinitely. In December 1960, Nikkatsu added Shishido to the star rotation and redubbed it the "New Diamond Line," but in January 1961 Ishihara broke his leg skiing and did not return to the cameras for seven months. Then in February Akagi died after a go-cart crash on a Nikkatsu back lot – and, at the age of twenty-one, became Japan's answer to James Dean. To fill these gaps, Nikkatsu ramped up Kobayashi's production schedule, while giving Shishido more starring roles. Hideaki Nitani, an actor with a quick tongue and pop crooner looks, also helped take up the slack, though his moment at the top was brief.

Yet another up and comer was Hideki Takahashi, who had joined Nikkatsu in May 1961, while still in high school, and made his film debut three months later. He was cast in starring roles in 1962, but was not counted as a member of the New Diamond Line (i.e. Ishihara, Kobayashi, Shishido, Nitani and Wada). Instead he was lumped into the Green Line of new youth film (*seishun eiga*) stars, including Mitsuo Hamada, Sayuri Yoshinaga, and Masako Izumi.

Even so, the studio saw Takahashi as action movie material and gave him the lead in the film Akagi was shooting at the time of his accident, *The Man Who Lives in the Torrent* (*Gekiryu ni Ikiru Otoko*, 1962). It was a success and Takahashi started appearing in more action, and fewer youth film, roles.

In 1962 Kobayashi made two more instalments of the *Wanderer* series, while Ishihara and Asaoka starred in Koreyoshi Kurahara's *Ginza Love Story* (*Ginza no Koi no Monogatari*). Ishihara plays an artist whose fiancée (Asaoka) loses her memory in an accident and disappears from sight. The film became the year's sixth highest grosser and its theme song, a chart-topping hit and later a karaoke evergreen. It also marked the start of another Nikkatsu sub-genre – "mood action" (*mudo akushon*) or melodramas with action elements, usually pairing Ishihara and Asaoka as star-crossed lovers.

Nikkatsu's big prestige film of the year, however, was Kiriro Urayama's *Foundry Town* (*Cupola no Aru Machi*) – a drama about the troubled family life of a bright, spunky teenage girl in a rough factory town. Urayama's first film, with a script by Shohei Imamura, *Foundry Town* was ranked second in the *Kinema Junpo* magazine's annual critics poll. Sayuri Yoshinaga, who played the lead, became a major Nikkatsu star, appearing in a series of teen romances with Mitsuo Hamada.

By 1963 Nikkatsu's borderless action films were starting to fade at the box office, as Toei's new action genre – *ninkyo* ("chivalry") films – began to draw fans. Mostly set in the seventy-year period from the end of feudalism to the start of World War II, these films told simple stories of gangster heroes nobly upholding the *giri-ninjo* code of duty and self-sacrifice, against impossible odds. Nikkatsu had been making films along similar lines, starting with Toshio Masuda's 1962 hit *Hana and Ryu* (*Hana to Ryu*), but Toei set the pace – and Nikkatsu found itself playing catch up.

In 1963 Hideki Takahashi starred in *Symbol of a Man* (*Otoko no Monsho*), the first of a ten-part *ninkyo* film series that ran until 1966. Takahashi played a pure-hearted young doctor who is drawn, against his will, into the world of his gang boss father. Takahashi's straight-arrow screen persona was a perfect fit for the series and Takahashi soon became a mainstay of Nikkatsu's *ninkyo* film line-up, though Kobayashi, Shishido and Ishihara also made films in the genre.

Nikkatsu's biggest hit of 1963, however, was Shohei Imamura's *The Insect Woman* (*Nippon Konchuki*), a drama of a rural woman's bitter struggle for survival. The year's highest domestic grosser, the film also topped the *Kinema Junpo* critics poll. Imamura, who had joined Nikkatsu in 1954 from Shochiku, made one more film, *Intentions of Murder* (*Akai Satsui*, 1964), for the studio before leaving to become an independent.

Ishihara, still the studio's biggest star, was in transition, moving from the young rebel roles of his early career to the more mature characters of his mood action films. In 1963, he also launched his own production company, Ishihara Production, though he stayed with Nikkatsu another four years, until 1967.

Compared with the blistering pace of his early Nikkatsu years, Ishihara made fewer films in this period, twenty six, starting with the 1963 New Year's release *Hana and Ryu* (*Hana to Ryu*). Among the most popular was *Red Handkerchief* (*Akai Handkerchief*, 1964) – Toshio Masuda's mood action classic starring Ishihara as a detective who shoots and kills an escaping witness – the father of a girl (Ruriko Asaoka) he loves.

Another hit that year was Buichi Saito's *Looking at Love and Death* (*Ai to Shi o Mitsumete*), starring Sayuri Yoshinaga as a girl valiantly battling illness and falling in love with a fellow sufferer (Mitsuo Hamada). Audiences wept buckets and the film finished number two at the domestic box office for 1964, behind Kon Ichikawa's controversial documentary about the Tokyo Olympics.

Seeking to appeal less to the heart than the loins was Seijun Suzuki's *Gate of Flesh* (*Nikutai no Mon*, 1964), a remake of a 1948 Masahiro Makino film. Joe Shishido stars as a cynical ex-soldier who takes up with a gang of colourfully attired whores scraping out a living in the early-post-war ruins. It was a hit with fans – and became Shishido's favourite among his Nikkatsu films.

By this time, however, the Japanese film industry was in crisis, as its audience migrated to television en masse. In 1964 admissions totalled 510 million, only 45.3 percent of the all-time high of 1,127.4 million in 1958, while the number of theatres declined to 5,366, compared with 7,457 at the 1960 peak.

Toei survived this crunch with its popular gang films, targeted at the young men flooding into the universities, factories and offices to build Japan's economic miracle. Under producer Koji Shundo, the studio churned out one hit series after another set in Japan's underworld, the box office leader being Teruo Ishii's *Abashiri Prison* (*Abashiri Bangaichi*) series about the lives of convicts on the inside and outside of Japan's most famous prison.

Nikkatsu, however, was struggling to make action hits, let alone series. In 1965 and 1966 no Nikkatsu film was able to crack the domestic box office top ten. The studio released the highest-grossing domestic film of 1967 (though it actually opened early in 1968): Kei Kumai's *Tunnel to the Sun* (*Kurobe no Taiyo*). But this big-budget drama about the building of the massive Kurobe Dam in Toyama Prefecture – a project that took hundreds of lives – was not made by Nikkatsu, but the production companies of its two stars: Yujiro Ishihara and Toshiro Mifune. Its success would encourage Ishihara in his quest for independence from the studio that had nurtured him.

Taking up much of the slack of Ishihara's absence was Akira Kobayashi, Nikkatsu's most reliable action star. Since the late 1950s, he had continued to make the studio's signature borderless action films – twenty six altogether in the years 1963 to 1967 – while branching out into *ninkyo* films, appearing in nine in the same period. But unlike Ishihara, Takahashi and Shishido, Kobayashi never felt the need to reinvent himself: He was still the same unpretentious, unflappable, unstoppable Akira as ever, though he bulked up as he aged, becoming even more of a macho presence.

This consistency, as well as his steady popularity, made Kobayashi ideally suited to series work. In addition to the *Wanderer*, *Drifter* and *'Mite Guy* series of his

Original theatrical poster for Yasuharu Hasebe's "Slaughter Gun" (Minagoroshi no Kenju, 1967).

early stardom, Kobayashi appeared in the eight-part *Gambler* series from 1964 to 1966, playing a gambling wonder who can perform miracles with dice.

From 1966 to 1967 he also starred in the four-part *That Guy* (*Aitsu*) series as a gang lieutenant who becomes fed up with the yakuza life and decides to go straight. He hooks up with a traveling *enka* singer (comedian Tokyo Bonta), who becomes his comic sidekick. In the second instalment, *That Guy Is Tough* (*Fujimi na Aitsu*, 1967), Kobayashi reunited with *Wanderer* series director Buichi Saito and co-star Ruriko Asaoka, playing a former girlfriend.

Toward the end of his Nikkatsu career Kobayashi starred in yet another series, *Women's Cop* (*Onna no Keisatsu*, 1969-1970), playing a scout and enforcer for Ginza bars and cabarets. His vigorous protection of his girls against gangsters, pimps and other undesirables earns him the nickname "*Women's Cop*". The focus in this four-part series was more on eroticism than action, however.

Kobayashi alone could not keep the Nikkatsu Action production line humming, however. He – and the studio – needed help. Nikkatsu had tried to find it in Hideaki Nitani, but after starring in several action films in 1961 and 1962, he had returned to supporting parts. Though an intelligent and adaptable actor, Nitani was finally too bland a presence to carry a film on his own.

Joe Shishido was a different story. Though he had become popular playing bad guys, with an insouciance that verged on self-parody, Shishido could, as Nitani could not, also be a convincing tough guy hero. From 1963 to 1967 he cultivated this side of his screen persona, playing the lead in nine action films and a second lead in sixteen more, for a total of twenty five.

Among his better films of this period was Seijun Suzuki's *Youth of the Beast* (*Yaju no Seishun*), in which Suzuki first fully unleashed the playfully surreal, blackly humourous style that was to make him a cult sensation. Though Shishido's performance as a cop on a mission had its comic touches (including a memorable scene in which his puffy face was squashed like a water balloon against a pane of glass), his character spent much of the film in a hard-boiled mode, as he went undercover to discover the truth about a superior's mysterious double suicide with a call girl.

Shishido continued to venture into the dark underside of contemporary Japanese life, with comic interludes, but his true arrival as a hard-boiled star came in 1967 with his roles in Takashi Nomura's *A Colt Is My Passport* (*Colt wa Ore no Passport*), Suzuki's *Branded to Kill* (*Koroshi no Rakuin)* and Yasuharu Hasebe's *Slaughter Gun* (*Minagoroshi no Kenju*) – a trio of films that were career high points.

Despite his rise in the studio hierarchy, Shishido never had the box office clout of Ishihara and Kobayashi at their peaks. He certainly could not save *Branded to Kill* – which not only flopped, but so baffled Nikkatsu president Kyusaku Hori that he fired Suzuki – who did not make another feature film for a decade. Nikkatsu clearly needed another action star, even if a return to the glory days of the Diamond Line was out of the question.

It found one in Tetsuya Watari, who was scouted in the studio cafeteria in 1965, before he could even take an audition. Though blessed with long legs and good looks reminiscent of the young Ishihara, Watari came along at a different, difficult moment, when the Japanese film industry was in steep decline and the culture was about to undergo massive change. Instead of cruising the Shonan Coast, college students were about to put on helmets and pick up staves to battle riot police.

Watari got off to a fast start, appearing with Ishihara in two films – *I'll Make You Cry* (*Nakaseru ze*, 1965) and *Duel in the Red Valley* (*Akai Tanima no Ketto*, 1966), as well as starring in remakes of four Ishihara hits, including *The Guy Who Started a Storm* (*Arashi o Yobu Otoko*, 1966), *Stars, Don't Weep: The Winner* (*Hoshi Yo Nagekuna: Shori No Otoko*, 1967), *A Slope in the Sun* (*Hi no Ataru Sakamichi*, 1967) and *Velvet Hustler* (*Kurenai no Nagareboshi*, 1967).

The most enduring of this lot – and Watari's own favourite – was the last, Toshio Masuda's loose remake of his own 1958 hit *Red Quay* (*Akai Hatoba*). Though usually a serious type, on and off the screen, Watari shone as an impudent hitman modelled on Jean-Paul Belmondo's character in *Breathless*. Hiding out in Kobe after a job, he tries to seduce an equally impudent rich girl who is searching for her jewel dealer fiancé, but doesn't seem overly upset by his unexplained disappearance.

Watari finally carved out his own star identity in the *Hoodlum* (*Burai*) series, whose six instalments ran from 1968 to 1969. Based on the memoirs of real-life gangster Goro Fujita, the *Hoodlum* films are distinct from both *ninkyo* films and the more realistic gang films Kinji Fukasaku was to make at Toei in the early 1970s. Playing a street tough whose weapon of choice was a short sword, Watari was nonetheless a sympathetic sort, who may have been a lone wolf, but was not, like several of Fukasaku's heroes, crazed with rage, lust or some combination thereof.

Abroad, Watari is best known for his work in Suzuki's *Tokyo Drifter* (*Tokyo Nagaremono*, 1966). The story, of a gangster who tries defend his former boss against the murderous intentions of yakuza rivals and ends up on the run for his own life, is a genre standard, but in Suzuki's hands becomes a comically bizarre send-up of genre conventions. Watari, however, plays it straight from beginning to end, while bursting forth with the infectious theme song at every opportunity.

From 1968 to 1971, the studio shifted production to what came to be called Nikkatsu New Action. Although featuring studio regulars Kobayashi, Shishido and Watari, New Action films brought new stars, directors and approaches to the studio's action product. Their attempt to reflect 1960s styles and trends – including

Original theatrical poster for Yasuharu Hasebe's "Retaliation" (Shima wa Moratta, 1968).

more explicit violence and sex and a more assertive role for women – did not often translate into big hits, but several New Action film have become cult classics.

Among them were the five films of the *Stray Cat Rock* (*Nora Neko Rock*) series, which became cult favourites both in Japan and abroad. (One fan, Quentin Tarantino, incorporated motifs from the *Stray Cat Rock* series into *Kill Bill: Vol. 1*.) Also, New Action stars Tatsuya Fuji, Yoshio Harada and Meiko Kaji, as well as New Action directors Yasuharu Hasebe, Keiichi Ozawa, Yukihiro Sawada and Toshiya Fujita went on to long post-Nikkatsu careers.

Compared with the first wave of Nikkatsu Action films a decade earlier, New Action product tended to be cruder and ruder, trending, in the end, to outright exploitation. The films did not centre on noble drifters, but dirty heroes fighting for survival or gangs of punks looking for kicks. The women in their lives were no longer angels in kimono or fashionable, fast-talking modern girls (both types played by Ruriko Asaoka), but long-haired panthers in mini-dresses (usually played by Meiko Kaji).

Also, instead of rugged individualists modelled on the cowboys and private detectives of Hollywood, the heroes and their women usually ran with other delinquents, with jeeps and bikes being favoured forms of transportation. Their adventures often unfolded in "international" settings, such as foreigner-frequented clubs or back roads around US military bases that were not specifically Japanese or foreign – but somewhere in between. In other words, squarely in the borderless action tradition.

During this period Nikkatsu was also churning out *ninkyo* films, in a head-to-head competition with arch-rival Toei, while continuing to make youth dramas, comedies and even traditional Nikkatsu Action films. In the late 1960s, New Action films accounted for a relatively small part of its total output.

As the 1960s gave way to the 1970s, and Nikkatsu's older stars, including Ishihara and Asaoka, moved on to new opportunities in television and elsewhere, the studio upped production of New Action films with new stars like Kaji, Fuji and Harada, reasoning that fresh faces would draw the all-important younger audience.

It was a member of the old guard, Kobayashi, who made the biggest early contribution to the New Action genre, however, starting with hard-boiled gangster films like Hasebe's *Retaliation* (*Shima wa Moratta*, 1968), *Roughneck* (*Arakure*, 1969) and *Bloody Territories* (*Koiki Boryoku: Ryuketsu No Shima*, 1969). Shishido was also a prominent New Action star, though during this period he was scaling back his Nikkatsu work in favour of television.

Meanwhile, Watari's career was on the rise, launched by the popular *Hoodlum* series (1968-69) that defined the early New Action style. In 1970 and 1971, as New

Action moved into its later phase, he was the genre's most familiar face, though he stood apart from its Age of Aquarius group ethos, ever the stoic loner.

Another New Action regular was Tatsuya Fuji, who had struggled through the ranks after joining Nikkatsu in 1962, but got breakthrough roles as wild-at-heart gangsters in Hasebe's *Roughneck* and *Bloody Territories*. In 1970 and 1971 Fuji starred in the *Stray Cat Rock* series, playing a biker gang leader who indulges every appetite and impulse, sexual or sadistic, but is charismatic – and dangerous – enough to control his unruly underlings.

The first instalment, Hasebe's *Woman Boss: Stray Cat Rock* (*Onna Bancho: Nora Neko Rock*), starred tomboyish pop singer Akiko Wada in her film debut, and was produced by her agency, Hori Pro. A delinquent in real life before she began her singing career, Wada was credible as the leader of a girl biker gang that faces down the yakuza.

She proved to be a one-shot, however – and the role of series heroine passed to co-star Meiko Kaji, who had entered Nikkatsu in 1965 under her birth name, Masako Ota, but changed to Meiko Kaji in 1969. She was often cast in Nikkatsu's *ninkyo* and New Action films, but the *Stray Cat Rock* series made her a star.

Unlike Toei's star woman warrior Junko Fuji, who played the traditional ideal of Japanese womanhood – graceful, demure and kimonoed – even while slicing up gangsters with a short sword, Kaji was a dark, fiery, totally contemporary presence. Whether rumbling, riding motorbikes, or wearing extreme early 1970s fashions (maxi-coats! big floppy hats!), Kaji never looked less than cool, while dominating all but the most alpha males – to whom she extended a grudging respect as kings to her queen in the urban jungle.

She and her New Action co-stars couldn't stop Nikkatsu's downward box office slide, however. In June 1970 the studio and rival Daiei launched Daiichi Film Distribution, a joint venture charged with controlling distribution costs. The red ink proved hard to staunch, however, and in November 1971 Daiei ceased film production. Nikkatsu did as well in August, but restarted in November under new management and with a new line of erotic films, called Nikkatsu *roman poruno* ("romantic pornography"), which had real plots and characters, but simulated sex, with the critical parts carefully concealed. Though mild by the standards of *Deep Throat*, Roman Porno films attracted the attention of the Tokyo Metropolitan Police, which seized two of them in January 1972.

Despite this and other harassment from the authorities, Nikkatsu continued to make Roman Porno films until 1988, when the flood of cheaply made video porn made the genre too unprofitable to sustain. During this period the studio hired many aspiring young filmmakers who later rose to prominence as directors, including Yoshimitsu Morita, Yojiro Takita, Hidehiro Ito, Shun Nakahara, Takashi

Ishii, Yoichi Sai, Shusuke Kaneko and Yoichi Higashi. It also offered young directors like Tatsumi Kumashiro, Chusei Sone and Masaru Konuma opportunities to do taboo-challenging work, usually involving varieties of rough sex and S&M, that won critical acclaim.

Kumashiro, in particular, became a regular on the *Kinema Junpo* annual Best Ten critics' list with *Ichijo Sayuri: Flowing Desire* (*Ichijo Sayuri: Nureta Yokujo*, 1972), *The World of Geisha* (*Yojohan: Fusuma no Urabari*, 1973), *Bitterness of Youth* (*Seishun no Satetsu*, 1974) and *The Woman with Red Hair* (*Akai Kami no Onna*, 1979).

After abandoning Roman Porno, Nikkatsu ventured into other businesses, such as cable and satellite broadcasting, but found profits elusive. Its 80th anniversary film, the World War II drama *The Setting Sun* (*Rakuyo*, 1992), was a disaster at the box office, despite the presence of Diane Lane and Donald Sutherland in the cast, earning back only a small fraction of its twenty-plus million dollar budget. In 1993 Nikkatsu filed for bankruptcy protection. In 1996 game maker Namco bought the studio and began a restructuring program.

Today Nikkatsu operates the Nikkatsu Studio in the Tokyo suburb of Chofu, the Neco and Rainbow cable and satellite channels and the Cine Libre theatre chain, with theatres in Tokyo, Osaka, Kobe and Hakata. Since resuming film production in 1997 with the Kei Kumai melodrama *To Love* (*Ai Suru*), Nikkatsu has been releasing Japanese films, together with European, US and other foreign titles.

To celebrate its 90th anniversary the company produced the period drama *The Sea Is Watching* (*Umi wa Miteita*), directed by Kei Kumai from a script by Akira Kurosawa, and *Aiki*, a drama about a disabled martial artist scripted and directed by Daisuke Tengan, the son of Shohei Imamura. Both films were considerably cheaper to make than *The Setting Sun* – and avoided its dire box office fate.

In the new millennium Nikkatsu has produced everything from Naomi Kawase's family drama *Shara* (*Sharasoju*) to Ryuhei Kitamura's martial arts actioner *Alive* and Takashi Shimizu's horror hit *Juon: The Grudge* (*Juon*). Among its newer titles is Hideyuki Hirayama's *Lady Joker* (2004), a drama of corporate wrongdoing and victims' revenge starring Tetsuya Watari, in his first Nikkatsu film in nearly three decades.

In September 2005, Index Corp., a telecom company that provides mobile phone and Internet contents, bought a majority stake in Nikkatsu from Namco. Index has plans for exploiting Nikkatsu's library of nearly 7,000 films on TV, mobile phones, the Internet and video-on-demand, while financing new Nikkatsu films and expanding Nikkatsu's overseas sales network. Nikkatsu will not recover its old glory under new ownership – the days of the Diamond Line are long gone – but Nikkatsu Action will continue to survive and thrive on DVD – or whatever format replaces it.

Akira Kobayashi *(below right)* faces off in "Roughneck" (Arakure, 1969).

THE NIKKATSU ACTION BIG THREE, PLUS ONE: ISHIHARA, KOBAYASHI, AKAGI and WATARI

Yujiro Ishihara (1934-1987)

He was called the "Tough Guy," a symbol of Japanese macho for more than three decades. In his later years, with his puffy jowls, paunch and gravely voice, Yujiro Ishihara was a stolid figure who looked as though he had drained too many glasses of Chivas. Still tough, but in a battle-weary, middle-aged way.

The "Tough Guy" hadn't started out so tough, however. In 1956, when he appeared in his first film, Takumi Furukawa's *Season of the Sun* (*Taiyo no Kisetsu*), Yujiro was a tall, gangly college boy with a cheerful impudence and zero acting experience.

The movie, which featured Yujiro in bit role as a school boxing club friend of the hero, was a big hit, mainly for its then scandalous treatment of youthful sex and violence on the Shonan Coast near Tokyo, which promptly became a magnet for youth seeking the former.

Though Yujiro had only a bit role, the women in the audience couldn't take their eyes off his long, lanky legs – then an uncommon sight in Japan. He projected a youthful charm and sexual confidence that bordered on arrogance – and spelled star charisma.

Yujiro got the role through a family connection – his older brother Shintaro had written the novel on which the film was based. (Shintaro later became a right-wing politician and commentator and is currently governor of Tokyo.) Still a student at Keio University in Tokyo, Yujiro was regarded as the representative of the book and film's "Sun Tribe" (*Taiyozoku*) by fans.

The Sun Tribe were kids who had grown up in post-war Japanese society, in all its chaos and freedom. Instead of slaving for a company, they wanted to hang out on the Ginza or at the beach, listening to groovy jazz sounds and working on their attitudes. Their elders regarded them as spoiled and wild; they couldn't have cared less. They were the Japanese counterparts of another Sun Tribe on the opposite side of the Pacific then creating the culture of surfing, hot-rodding, and fun, fun, fun in the warm California sun.

Yujiro later claimed to be embarrassed by his media image as a Sun Tribe chieftain. In a 1958 book entitled *The Story of My Youth* (*Waga Seishun Monogatari*) he wrote that "compared with other teenagers today I feel that I'm rather old-fashioned."

Old-fashioned or not, Yujiro was a gilded youth compared with most of his contemporaries. His father had been a shipbuilding company executive and, though he had died when Yujiro and Shintaro were still young, his sons had grown up relatively unaffected by the hardships of the early post-war years. Shintaro had attended Hitotsubashi University and Yujiro had been admitted to Keio University from its affiliated high school, without having to sweat through entrance exams. Both were elite private institutions – the Japanese equivalent of the Ivy League.

Instead of grinding away at the books, Yujiro spent his college days sailing his boat off the Zushi Coast, playing sports and drinking with his friends at university bars. A typical Keio student, in other words, but one with uncommon good looks (though his teeth needed the attention of a good orthodontist).

Yujiro Ishihara takes on a gang in "Tomorrow Tomorrow's Wind Will Come" (Ashita wa Ashita no Kaze ga Fuku, 1958).

His first leading role was in Ko Nakahira's *Crazed Fruit* (*Kurutta Kajitsu*, 1956), playing a jaded, sybaritic Shonan youth who discovers that the seemingly innocent girl (Mie Kitahara) his unworldly younger brother is crazy about is in fact secretly married to a middle-aged American. He proceeds to steal the girl away from both, with tragic consequences. The film was enthusiastically praised by François Truffaut, then an influential young film critic, who recommended its preservation in the Cinémathèque Française film archive. In Japan, it became a controversial hit, as did the Hawaiian-flavoured theme song, sung by Yujiro in his light, warm baritone – a voice that was to deepen and become familiar to millions of Japanese.

The film and the *succès de scandale* that accompanied it launched Yujiro to stardom: he became Japan's Elvis and James Dean rolled into one – a generational hero and heartthrob. The Sun Tribe boom was brief, however. Adult guardians of public morals hated Sun Tribesmen and what they represented and their disapproval sent chills down the none-too-sturdy spines of studio executives. *Eirin* (Motion Picture Code of Ethics Committee), the industry censorship body, asked the studios to stop making Sun Tribe films and, after producing four of them, Nikkatsu complied, shutting down production of *The Gray Classroom* (*Haiiro no Kyoshitsu*), a film based on a Shintaro Ishihara novel.

For Yujiro, the Sun Tribe controversy was little more than a bump on the road to a fabulous career. From 1957 he churned out hits for Nikkatsu in a variety of genres, from melodrama to comedy, but it was as an action star that he made his biggest impact, under his new "Tough Guy" nickname.

In Umetsugu Inoue's *The Winner* (*Shorisha*, 1957), he played a punk kid who tries boxing as a lark, gets the tar punched out of him and starts training for real. In other words, the reverse of the usual hungry-underdog-battles-to-victory story. In Inoue's follow-up, *The Eagle and the Hawk* (*Washi to Taka*, 1957), Yujiro portrayed a seaman who joins the crew of a cargo ship with the aim of finding a man who drove his father to suicide. Once again his character's bad attitude gets him into trouble that he escapes with his fists.

His biggest hit of the year, however, was Inoue's *The Guy Who Started a Storm* (*Arashi o Yobu Otoko*, 1957). Yujiro played a wild kid whose ambition is to become a jazz drummer, but has more of a talent for trouble than rhythm. Released at the peak New Year's season, the film became the third biggest box-office hit of 1957. It inspired

above: Yujiro Ishihara and Mie Kitahara take five in "The Guy Who Started a Storm" (Arashi o Yobu Otoko, 1957).
opposite: Yujiro Ishihara crawls to safety in "The Winner" (Shorisha, 1957).

rock-concert reactions from audiences, who clapped and yelled when Yujiro sang about being "a drummer, a no-good drummer, when I get mad, I start a storm."

In addition to the veteran Inoue, Yujiro worked with a new crop of young Nikkatsu directors, who had joined the studio as assistant directors soon after it restarted production in 1954 and who jump-started the next, action-oriented phase of his career.

One was Koreyoshi Kurahara, whose directorial debut, *I Am Waiting* (*Ore wa Matteiru ze*, 1957), featured Yujiro as a boxer-turned-restaurant-manager who rescues a suicidal young woman (Mie Kitahara) one foggy night. The manager – who has a troubled past and lives for a dream that turns out to be a lie – is a darker, more conflicted character than those of Yujiro's Sun Tribe films.

Another young up-and-comer was Toshio Masuda, with whom Yujiro made twenty five films – the most of any Nikkatsu director – starting with Masuda's third feature, *Rusty Knife* (*Sabita Knife*, 1958). Based a script by Shintaro Ishihara, the film featured Yujiro and another rising Nikkatsu star, Akira Kobayashi, in their first on-screen pairing as former *chinpira* (apprentice gangsters) trying to restart their lives, while avoiding hoods who want to kill them for witnessing a hit.

His next film with Masuda, *Red Quay* (*Akai Hatoba*, 1958), further extended his romantic loner image. Set in Kobe, an international port city, the film was a reworking of *Pépé le Moko* that set the pattern for Nikkatsu's borderless action films for years to come. Yujiro plays a hitman who comes to Kobe to hide out with his hostess girlfriend after a job. There he falls for a girl (Mie Kitahara) who knows nothing of his occupation. He also becomes the target of an enemy gang – and a local detective who knows he is responsible for the Tokyo hit. Once again, Yujiro outfights and outwits everything but his lonely heart.

By the end of 1958, his stardom firmly established, Yujiro was ready to lead the Nikkatsu Action genre through its peak years, from 1959 to 1962. Or he was, rather, until he broke a leg skiing in January 1961 – a mishap that kept him away from the cameras for nearly seven months.

Even before the accident Yujiro was appearing in fewer action films – six in 1959, four in 1960, one in 1961 and four in 1962 – or less than half of his total output of thirty two in this period, which included so-called "youth films" (*seishun eiga*), melodramas and even four salaryman films.

In his action films of this period, Yujiro usually played a reporter, doctor, pilot, music producer or other holder of a steady job, with something resembling a normal life, not a hitman or other underworld type. This was consistent with his non-action roles, in which he portrayed more mature, if not always conventional, types. Yujiro, together with the teenage fans of his 1950s heyday, was growing up.

One of his better-remembered films from this period is Ko Nakahira's *Crimson Wings* (*Kurenai no Tsubasa*, 1959), with Yujiro playing a pilot who flies a pushy magazine writer (Sanae Nakahara) and mysterious businessman (Hideaki Nitani) to Hachijojima, an island south of Tokyo, together with a shipment of vaccine for a boy suffering from tetanus.

Midway, the businessman is revealed as a thief on the lam. He forces Yujiro to land on a small uninhabited island, where he is to be picked up by a boat. The resulting cat-and-mouse game between pilot and thief has its absurdities, mostly involving stunts with pistols, but it ends in triumph for Yujiro's pilot – an in-control pro, for whom outsmarting a desperate criminal is almost a form of relaxation.

In 1962, Yujiro began making "mood action" (*mudo akushon*) films – melodramas with an action element, usually co-starring Ruriko Asaoka. Among the most successful was Koreyoshi Kurahara's *Ginza Love Story* (*Ginza no Koi no Monogatari*, 1962). Yujiro plays a struggling artist living in a small Ginza flat with a moody jazz pianist (Jerry Fujio) and dating a pretty seamstress (Asaoka). Their romance has its bumps – the artist wants to pursue his art, the seamstress wants him to settle down – but is moving toward a happy ending when the seamstress is nearly killed crossing a street and disappears. Years later, she resurfaces – with no memory of the artist and their love.

The film takes unexpected turns and gives the two stars a chance to stretch beyond their usual on-screen images. It was the sixth biggest Japanese box office hit of the year and its theme song, sung over and over in the course of the film, became a chart-topping hit and a karaoke perennial.

Kurahara's follow-up, *That Despicable Guy* (*Nikui Anchikusho*, 1962) starred Yujiro and Asaoka as a couple – he a popular DJ, she his manager – who work together like a well-oiled machine, until he starts to chafe at her minute-by-minute schedule and the emptiness of their "perfect" relationship. On an impulse he answers an ad posted by a woman (Izumi Ashikawa) who wants a driver to deliver a jeep to her lover, a doctor (Asao Koike) in a remote Kyushu village. The DJ at first sees her story as something to pump for its human interest angle and discard, but he ends by volunteering to drive the jeep himself. Not only does he want to escape his pressure cooker life, but he also wants to prove to the woman and himself that he is still capable of an unselfish act. Shocked by what she sees as professional irresponsibility and personal betrayal, the manager follows after him in his sports car

Their various confrontations and adventures from Tokyo to Kyushu are the heart of the story – and helped make *That Despicable Guy* a stand-out among Nikkatsu's action product in general, and Yujiro's films specifically. It was also closer to the "real" Yujiro than any of his previous work.

From 1963 until 1967, when he left the studio, Yujiro appeared in twenty five Nikkatsu films – or twenty six counting his New Year's film for 1963, *Hana and Ryu* (*Hana to Ryu*), Toshio Masuda's reworking of a 1954 Toei film about the life and loves of a fiery young stevedore in Meiji-era (1868-1912) Kyushu. With Yujiro playing the lead, the film became the third biggest domestic hit of the year.

In these years Yujiro appeared in more mood action films – fifteen in all – while no longer making the melodramas and youth films that had largely defined the previous stage of his Nikkatsu career. Mood action films were basically romantic dramas with fist fights and gun play, and Yujiro, now advancing into his thirties, was too old for youth film roles.

One unusual – and unusually good – film from this period was Kon Ichikawa's *Alone on the Pacific* (*Taiheiyo Hitoribochi*, 1963), based on the true story of a young Japanese man who had sailed solo across the Pacific in 1962. Despite all the hardships of the film's 94-day voyage, including a typhoon and shortages of food and water, Yujiro's character toughed it out with a combination of grit and cool that bordered on the comic.

Another career landmark was Toshio Masuda's *Red Handkerchief* (*Akai Handkerchief*, 1964). In this ultimate mood action film Yujiro played a Yokohama detective who shoots and kills the father of a factory girl (Ruriko Asaoka) he has become infatuated with. The father, a humble *yatai* (food stall) owner, and witness in a big drug case, was trying to wrestle away the gun of Yujiro's partner (Hideaki Nitani) when Yujiro pulled the trigger.

Flash forward four years: Yujiro is a now construction worker, his partner a wealthy businessman who has married the factory girl – and has connections to the yakuza. In contrast, to the brash types he often played in his Sun Tribe films, Yujiro's character in *Red Handkerchief* is an embittered man, with no happy ending in sight. He returns to Yokohama and tries to learn the truth about what happened that fatal day, but the old cockiness is gone, replaced by a new gravitas.

Yet another mood action hit was Mitsuo Ezaki's *Black Strait* (*Kuroi Kaikyo*, 1964), starring Yujiro as a yakuza who has ascended the gang hierarchy by killing his boss's rival and taking the rap for it. As the movie begins, he is out of prison and eager to start a new life with the boss's daughter, a fashion designer who hates her father's world. The boss, however, is reluctant to let him go – and holds him by chains from the past that are not easily broken. Then the hero is ordered to kill again – but this time the target is another sub-boss who has betrayed the gang and reminds Yujiro uncomfortably of himself. His end is, rare for a Nikkatsu Action hero, a tragic one.

During his Nikkatsu years, Yujiro launched a second, highly successful career as a singer; one he was to pursue for the rest of his life. He released a total of 218 albums and 235 singles, mostly of soulful Japanese ballads called *enka*, and nearly all became big sellers.

Yujiro was also a trendsetter in his adoption of things new and Western. Off screen, he not only drove fancy foreign cars and wore expensive designer clothes – standard movie star stuff, even for 1950s Japan – but was also an expert skier and yachtsman, accomplishments then rare in a country still emerging from post-war poverty.

In 1963, with brother Shintaro at the helm, Yujiro sailed in the Transpacific Yacht Race aboard the thirty-nine-foot sloop Contessa III. The only Japanese boat in the 2,225 mile annual race, the Contessa III survived thirty-knot winds to finish second in its class. Yujiro returned home a hero, this time for real.

He also found the real thing in his off-screen romancing of frequent co-star Mie Kitahara. In January 1960 Yujiro and Mie flew to Hawaii on what the press dubbed a "secret honeymoon." Their lack of a marriage certificate, however, caused a scandal. Finally, in December, they were wed at the Nikkatsu Hotel, which was owned, conveniently enough, by the studio. One hundred guards patrolled the grounds during the four-hour ceremony to keep frenzied female fans from storming inside.

Original theatrical poster for Toshio Masuda's "Hana and Ryu" (Hana to Ryu, 1962).

While making news with his personal life, Yujiro was becoming restless with his studio servitude. In 1963, he started his own production company, Ishihara Production (now Ishihara International Productions). Its first film: *Alone on the Pacific*.

A brief sojourn in Hollywood in 1965 gave him another break from the Nikkatsu conveyor belt. He appeared in *Those Magnificent Men in Their Flying Machines*, a Twentieth Century Fox comedy about the early days of aviation starring Sarah Miles, Terry-Thomas, Robert Morley and Gert Frobe. Though the film was corny and coy, Yujiro acquitted himself well, portraying an accident-prone air racer with an amused panache that defied then prevalent Hollywood stereotypes about Japanese.

In February of that year, Yujiro made headlines of a different type when cops raided his house looking for pistols. An acquaintance who described himself as Yujiro's bodyguard had been arrested for selling smuggled guns to the yakuza and the police suspected that Yujiro was also involved. The search turned up nothing but a Japanese sword and the head of a lance – both lacking the necessary licences. Yujiro denied any connection with either the bodyguard or the gun-smuggling ring. Finally, in September, after lengthy and embarrassing questioning, the police cleared him of wrongdoing.

From 1968, Yujiro made more films with Ishihara Production and other outside companies, while cutting back on his work for Nikkatsu. One was *Tunnel to the Sun* (*Kurobe no Taiyo*, 1968), a drama based on a true-life story about a dangerous dam project, and *Safari 5000* (*Eiko e no 5000 Kilo*, 1969), in which he portrayed a driver in the Paris-Dakar Rally. Both were successes at the box office.

By the early 1970s, Yujiro, like so many other stars of his generation, found hits harder to come by. In 1971 he made his last film for Nikkatsu, Yasuharu Hasebe's gang epic *A Man's World* (*Otoko no Sekai*). In 1973, he starred in his last film for Ishihara Production, *Payback for Treachery* (*Hangyaku no Hoshu*), playing a man who joins with a freelance photographer (Tetsuya Watari) to take revenge on a drug boss.

After vowing that he would never appear in a TV series because of the cheesy quality of Japanese television, Yujiro succumbed in 1972, agreeing to play the lead in *Howl at the Sun* (*Taiyo ni Hoero*), a police detective series. The show, with its gun battles and high-speed car chases, may have stretched the limits of credibility (real Japanese cops avoid both like the plague), but it found favour with viewers and stayed on the air for fourteen years.

As Yujiro advanced into middle age, his smoking, drinking and partying to live up to his Tough Guy image began to take its toll. On 25 April, 1981 he collapsed on the set during the filming of another TV cop show, *Seibu Police* (*Seibu Keisatsu*). After being rushed to Keio Hospital, he was diagnosed with a heart aneurysm.

So many well-wishers descended on the hospital – 12,000 in all – that the hospital staff set up a tent outside to receive them. In addition to the usual flowers and folded-paper cranes – symbols of good fortune – fans sent 2,000 stuffed dolls and cakes, including one in the shape of a yacht, and 3,000 orders of sushi.

Yujiro recovered and returned to work, but fell victim to liver cancer. After a six-year battle, he succumbed on 17 July, 1987 at the age of fifty two. He left ¥1.748 billion in assets, including a thirty-room house in Tokyo's exclusive Seijo neighbourhood, a villa near Lake Yamanaka, and two homes in Hawaii. Within days after his death record stores had sold out their stocks of his records, including the entire pressing of new thirteen-album boxed set titled, simply, "The Big Man" (another of his nicknames), that contained 154 songs and cost a hefty ¥25,000.

Like Elvis and James Dean, Yujiro has become a Dead Legend, whose flame still burns brightly. His songs have become karaoke standards, his Nikkatsu films have been re-released on DVD and his company, Ishihara International Productions, is still going strong, headed by Tetsuya Watari, Yujiro's Nikkatsu "younger brother" and sometime co-star.

To ensure the flame never dies, the Yujiro Ishihara Memorial Hall has been built near the port of Otaru, Hokkaido where Yujiro and Shintaro were born and spent their early years. There visitors can see not only clips from Yujiro's films, TV shows and commercials, but also his memorabilia and a mock-up of the set from *Tunnel to the Sun*. They can even buy clothes modelled on Yujiro's own wardrobe. Not quite Graceland, perhaps – but a fitting tribute to Japan's biggest post-war star.

Yujiro Ishihara Selected Filmography

Season of the Sun (*Taiyo no Kisetsu*, 1956)
Crazed Fruit (*Kurutta Kajitsu*, 1956)
Human Torpedo Attack (*Ningengyorai Shutsugekisu*, 1956)
The Birth of the Jazz Girls (*Jazz Musume Tanjo*, 1956)
Lunar Eclipse (*Gesshoku*, 1957)
The Sun's Legend (*Bakumatsu Taiyoden*, 1957)
The Winner (*Shorisha* , 1957)
This Day's Life (*Kyo no Inochi*, 1957)
The Boys of the Sea (*Umi no Yarodomo*, 1957)
The Eagle and the Hawk (*Washi to Taka*, 1957)
I Am Waiting (*Ore wa Matteiru ze*, 1957)
The Guy Who Started a Storm (*Arashi o Yobu Otoko*, 1957)
A Slope in the Sun (*Hi no Ataru Sakamichi*, 1958)
Rusty Knife (*Sabita Knife*, 1958)
Run Into the Storm (*Arashi no Naka o Tsuppashire*, 1958)
Tomorrow Tomorrow's Wind Will Come (*Ashita wa Ahita no Kaze ga Fuku*, 1958)

Red Quay (Akai Hatoba, 1958)
Crimson Wings (Kurenai no Tsubasa, 1959)
Gangster Teacher (Yakuza Sensei, 1960)
Man at the Bullfight (Togyu ni Kakeru Otoko, 1960)
The Tree of Youth (Seinen no Ki, 1960)
He and I (Aitsu to Watashi, 1961)
A Bold Life (Dodotaru Jinsei, 1961)
The Arab Storm (Arab no Arashi, 1961)
The Young (Wakai Hito, 1962)
Ginza Love Story (Ginza no Koi no Monogatari, 1962)
That Despicable Guy (Nikui Anchikusho, 1962)
Hana and Ryu (Hana to Ryu, 1962)
Alone on the Pacific (Taiheiyo Hitoribochi, 1963)
Black Strait (Kuroi Kaikyo, 1964)
Red Handkerchief (Akai Handkerchief, 1964)
Those Magnificent Men in Their Flying Machines, or How I Flew from London to Paris in 25 hours 11 minutes (1965)
White Bird (Shirotori, 1965)
Duel in the Red Valley (Akai Tanima no Ketto, 1966)
The Harbour of No Return (Kaerazeru Hatoba, 1966)
Challenge to Glory (Eiko e no Chosen, 1966)
Hawk of the Quay (Hatoba no Taka, 1967)
Tunnel to the Sun (Kurobe no Taiyo, 1968)
Stormy Era (Showa no Inochi, 1968)
Under the Banner of Samurai (Furin Kazan, 1969)
Safari 5000 (Eiko e no 5,000 Kilo, 1969)
Tenchu! (Hitokiri,1969)
The Cleanup (Arashi no Yushatachi, 1969)
Ambush at Blood Pass (Machibuse, 1970)
One Soldier's Gamble (Aru Heishi no Kake, 1970)
Men and War (Senso to Ningen: Unmei no Jokyoku, 1970)
A Man's World (Otoko no Sekai, 1971)
Shadow Hunter (Kage Gari, 1972)
Shadow Hunter: Roaring Cannon (Kage Gari: Hoero Taiho, 1972)
Payback for Treachery (Hangyaku no Hoshu, 1973)
Space Pirate Captain Harlock: Arcadia of My Youth (Waga Seishun no Arcadia, 1982) (voice)

right: Yujiro Ishihara.

Akira Kobayashi (1937-)

A Nikkatsu Action mainstay for more than a decade, who evolved from teen sensation to reliable macho lead, Akira Kobayashi was born in 1937 in Setagaya Ward, Tokyo, the son of a lighting director. A child actor and a star judoist at Mejiro High School in Tokyo, he joined Nikkatsu in 1956 after passing the third New Faces audition, together with Hideaki Nitani. He made his screen debut in Yuzo Kawashima's *Hungry Spirit* (*Ueru Tamashi*, 1956) and appeared in a succession of minor roles. He first attracted attention for his performance as young gangster-turned-bartender to Yujiro Ishihara's bar manager in Toshio Masuda's *Rusty Knife* (*Sabita Knife*, 1958). That same year Nikkatsu launched a publicity campaign promoting Kobayashi, Tamio Kawachi and Tadao Sawamoto as "Nikkatsu's three bad boys."

Though initially regarded as a younger version of Ishihara, Kobayashi had a punkish working-class aura, together with a winning crinkly smile, that contrasted with Ishihara's Golden Boy sheen. He began to get larger roles, as a troubled youth in Seijun Suzuki's *The Spring That Didn't Come* (*Funihazushita Haru*, 1958) and as a boxer in Masuda's *Forget About Women* (*Onna o Wasurero*, 1959), while making an impression for his performance of the later film's theme song.

His big break came in Buichi Saito's *Leaving Tosa of the South* (*Nangoku Tosa o Ato ni Shite*, 1959), in which he portrayed an ex-con who returns to his mother in Kochi and tries to go straight, with the aim of marrying and settling down with his pure-hearted fiancée (Ruriko Asaoka). His old gang, however, wants him back and is determined to get him, by fair means or foul. Boosted by Peggy Hayama's hit recording of the title song, the movie became a box office success, as well as the template for Kobayashi's signature *Wanderer* (*Wataridori*) and *Drifter* (*Nagaremono*) series.

In the nine-part *Wanderer* series (1959-1962), Kobayashi played a wanderer on Japan's back roads with most of the accoutrements of a Western hero, from a horse to fringes, guitar and even a trusty bullwhip. He moseys into a town or ranch, sides with the good local folk against gangsters and other evildoers, and wins the affection of a local maiden, played in all but one instalment by Asaoka. He also finds a rival in Joe Shishido, playing his usual role as a scapegrace with a good heart. All but the last instalment were helmed by Buichi Saito.

The series reached its peak with the fifth entry, *Plains Wanderer* (*Daisogen no Wataridori*, 1960), in which Kobayashi's drifter takes the side of Ainu – Japan's aborigines – fighting a developer (Nobuo Kaneko) who wants to turn their land into an airstrip for tourists. First, though, he encounters Shishido, just out of prison

Nikkatsu's Akira Kobayashi in action.

and back to collect from the developer after taking the fall for a bank robbery they pulled seven years earlier. After some initial back-and-forth, the two men take a wary liking to each other, but Shishido goes over to the dark side, accepting a job as muscle for the developer.

Meanwhile, the niece (Asaoka) of an Ainu-friendly landowner falls for Kobayashi, but is engaged to the landowner's son. As it happens, an Ainu girl (Mari Shiraki) is in love with the son – and is thus on Kobayashi's side.

These complications makes for an engagingly twisty story, while Kobayashi and Shishido exchange snappy banter and slick moves with a can-you-top-this fluency.

Kobayashi's singing in this series made him a pop sensation, while his romance with co-star Asaoka made him hot copy for the weekly magazines – Japan's tabloids. When he married pop diva Hibari Misora in 1961, upsetting all expectations, the weeklies had another field day. (Asaoka exited the *Wataridori* series soon after.)

In marrying the biggest name in Japanese show business, who sold records and movie tickets at a furious pace, Kobayashi found himself battling a massive inferiority complex. He even publicly denounced acting as "unmanly" and set himself up as president of a production company. The marriage failed, however, and in 1965 Misora announced their divorce (though it was later revealed that the couple had never bothered to legalise their living arrangements).

Despite his personal troubles, Kobayashi continued working steadily for Nikkatsu. He starred in the five-instalment *Drifter* series (1960-1961), which had the same basic stranger-in-town premise as the *Wanderer* films. Once again, Asaoka played the girl who gets left behind and Shishido appears, first as a villain, and from the second instalment, in his more usual roles as rival/ally. All five films were directed by Tokujiro Yamazaki.

Kobayashi also played the title character in the six-instalment *Ginza 'Mite Guy* (*Ginza Maitogai*, 1959-1963) series, a tough guy of unfixed occupation who battles various urban underworld types. In the first instalment, *Ginza 'Mite Guy*, released right after *Leaving Tosa of the South*, he comes to the aid of Asaoka, who is searching for her father's enemies – a four-man gang led by Nobusuke Ashida. During the war in China they swindled him out of a huge sum of money and their boss is now running a big Ginza cabaret. The hero gets close to him by posing as, of all things, an interior designer.

In 1963 the borderless action boom Kobayashi had helped so much to create faded at the box office, as competition from Toei's *ninkyo* films intensified. Kobayashi successfully switched to gangster roles, moving in the course of the decade, from the boyish hood of Suzuki's *Kanto Wanderer* (*Kanto Mushuku*, 1963) and *The Flower and the Angry Waves* (*Hana to Doto*, 1964) to the more rugged yakuza of Yasuharu Hasebe's *Retaliation* (*Shima wa Moratta*, 1968), *Roughneck* (*Arakure*, 1969) and *Bloody Territories* (*Koiki Boryoku: Ryuketsu no Shima*, 1969).

Among his most unusual and best known films from this period is Yasuharu Hasebe's *Black Tight Killers* (*Ore ni Sawaru to Abunai ze*, 1966). Kobayashi plays a photographer back from the Vietnam War. While at dinner with a pretty flight attendant (Chieko Matsubara) he met on the return flight from Vietnam, he becomes aware of a skulking foreigner who seems to have evil intentions against his date. Before he can find out exactly what they are, the foreigner is attacked by a gang of girls in black tights, armed with bubble-gum bullets and throwing blades in their compacts. The foreigner ends up dead and, while the photographer is phoning the cops, the flight attendant is kidnapped.

What's all the hullabaloo about? The flight attendant's deceased father returned from Okinawa after World War II with a large haul of Imperial Army gold. He hid it – and now a gang of Japanese yakuza and American crooks are after it. Meanwhile, a gang of female martial artists from Okinawa – the tights wearers – are going for the gold as well. Kobayashi gamely goes through his paces, while the candy-coloured, go-go, James Bond-ish action unfolds around him.

Another Hasebe film, *Roughneck*, gives fuller play to both the comic and serious sides of his tough guy persona. Kobayashi begins the film as a stone-broke hoodlum, finagling his way out of the train fare at a provincial station. He has come to find an *ototobun* (junior gangster, played by Tatsuya Fuji) living in town. Both, it turns out, have been bailed out of jail by Fuji's disapproving sister (Masako Izumi). Kobayashi soon takes up with a hot springs geisha (Yoko Machida), the lover of a local boss, whose gang is battling stiff competition from an outside rival. The newcomers, a Kansai syndicate, are scheming to take over a local quarry for a leisure development.

This sort of situation is also found in the *Wanderer* series, but instead of being on the side of the angels, as he would have been in a *Wanderer* film, the quarry owner is in cahoots with the local yakuza. Also, instead of protecting the weak, Kobayashi's hood wants to join whichever side promises the bigger payoff. He offers to work as a hitman for the newcomers – but his real aim is their safe, stuffed with loot.

While broadening his range in these and other roles, Kobayashi remained focused on his – and the studio's – bread-and-butter series work. From 1964 to 1966 he starred in the eight-part *Gambler* series as a professional gambler who can work miracles with dice, but can't always save lovers and siblings from his enemies. From 1966 to 1967 he also appeared in the four-part *That Guy* (*Aitsu*) series as a gangster-gone-straight who has adventures with an *enka* (Japanese ballad) singer sidekick, played by comedian Tokyo Bonta. In the second instalment, *That Guy Is Tough* (*Fujimi na Aitsu*, 1967), Kobayashi reunites with *Wanderer* series director Buichi Saito and co-star Ruriko Asaoka, playing a former girlfriend.

Original theatrical poster for "Women's Cop" (Onna no Keisatsu, 1969).

Akira Kobayashi.

From 1969 to 1970 Kobayashi headlined the four-part *Women's Cop (Onna no Keisatsu)* series. Playing a scout and enforcer for Ginza bars and cabarets, he is so zealous at saving girls from gangsters, pimps and other undesirables that he acquires the nickname Women's Cop. Once alone with his charges, however, he could become unprofessionally amorous.

As Nikkatsu's fortunes declined, Kobayashi remained commendably loyal, but in 1972, after the studio started producing its new line of *roman poruno* erotic features, he moved to Toei, then at the start of the boom for its *jitsuroku* ("true story") gang films. He played a calculating, cold-blooded yakuza boss in Kinji Fukasaku's *Battles Without Honour and Humanity 3: Proxy War (Jingi Naki Tatakai 3: Dairi Senso*, 1973), and *Battles Without Honour and Humanity: Police Tactics (Jingi Naki Tatakai: Chojo Sakusen*, 1974).

In the late 1970s, when the popularity of "true story" gangster films faded, Kobayashi concentrated on his singing career, television work and various business interests. In the 1990s, he returned to films, appearing in Seiji Izumi's *Legend of Carnage (Shuraba no Densetsu*, 1992) and *Emperor of Violence (Minbo no Teio*, 1993), and Shigeru Ishihara's *The Road to Bossdom (Don e no Michi*, 2003). Abroad he is best known for his Suzuki and Fukasaku films, with Hong Kong star Chow Yun-Fat claiming him as an influence, particularly in Chow's portrayal of a cool killer in John Woo's *A Better Tomorrow*.

Akira Kobayashi Selected Filmography

Hungry Spirit (Ueru Tamashi, 1956)
This Day's Life (Kyo no Inochi, 1957)
The Sun's Legend (Bakumatsu Taiyoden, 1957)
Rusty Knife (Sabita Knife, 1958)
False Step Spring (Funihazushita Haru, 1958)
Forget About Women (Onna o Wasurero, 1959)
Leaving Tosa of the South (Nangoku Tosa o Ato ni Shite, 1959)
Ginza 'Mite Guy (Ginza Maitogai, 1959)
Guitar Wanderer (Guitar o Motta Wataridori, 1959)
A Friendship That Started a Storm (Arashi o Yobu Yujo, 1959)
Gangster Song (Yakuza no Uta, 1960)
Plains Wanderer (Daisogen no Wataridori, 1960)
The Drifter Who Came from the Sea (Umi Kara Kita Nagaremono, 1960)
Runner in the Sun (Taiheiyo no Katsugiya, 1961)
The Jet That Flies Into the Storm (Arashi o Tsukkiru Jetto-ki, 1961)
The Wanderer Who Crossed the Waves (Hato o Koeru Wataridori, 1961)
Kanto Wanderer (Kanto Mushuku, 1963)
The Flower and the Angry Waves (Hana to Doto, 1964)

The Guy with No Home Town (*Yaro ni Kokyo wa Nai*, 1965)
Heart Won by Heart (*Iki-ni Kanzu*, 1965)
The Endless Duel (*Ketto*, 1967)
Three Seconds Before the Explosion (*Bakuhatsu Sanbyomae*, 1967)
Duel in the Storm (*Arashi no Hatashijo*, 1968)
Retaliation (*Shima wa Moratta*, 1968)
Older Sister (*Anego*, 1969)
Roughneck (*Arakure*, 1969)
Women's Cop (*Onna no Keisatsu*, 1969)
Women's Cop 2 (*Onna no Keisatsu 2*, 1969)
Bloody Territories (*Koiki Boryoku: Ryuketsu no Shima*, 1969)
Exiled to Hell (*Jigoku no Hamonjo*, 1969)
100 Gamblers (*Bakuto Hyakunin*, 1969)
Yakuza Wanderer: Bad Guys' Work (*Yakuza Wataridori: Akuto Kagyo*, 1969)
Appointment with Danger (*Onna no Keisatsu, Kokusaisen Machiaishitsu*, 1970)
Swirling Butterflies (*Onna no Keisatsu, Moderato*, 1970)
Battles Without Honour and Humanity 3: Proxy War (*Jingi Naki Tatakai 3: Dairi Senso*, 1973)
Battles Without Honour and Humanity: Police Tactics (*Jingi Naki Tatakai: Chojo Sakusen*, 1974)
Gate of Youth (*Seishun no Mon*, 1975)
Japan's Violent Archipelago: Killer Gang from Keihanshin (*Nikon Boryoku Retto: Keihanshin Koroshi no Gunman*, 1975)
True Story Postscript: Shock Strategy (*Jitsuroku Gaiden: Osaka Dengeki Sakusen*, 1976)
Hiroshima Chivalry: Hostage Rescue Strategy (*Hiroshima Jingi: Hitojichi Dakkai Sakusen*, 1976)
Tarao Bannai (1978)
Tarao Bannai: The Tragedy of Kimen Village (*Tarao Bannai: Kimen Mura no Sangeki*, 1978)
Conquest (*Seiha*, 1982)
Legend of Carnage (*Shuraba no Densetsu*, 1992)
Emperor of Violence (*Minbo no Teio*, 1993)
The Road to Bossdom (*Don e no Michi*, 2003)

right: Akira Kobayashi and equine companion in "Plains Wanderer" (Daisogen no Wataridori, 1960).

Keiichiro Akagi (1939-1961)

Often called "the Japanese James Dean" for both his moody, sensitive aura and his manner of death – driving too fast and recklessly, at the age of 21 – Keiichiro Akagi was in other ways not like Dean at all. Instead of playing confused adolescents battling parents, authorities and their own wayward impulses, Akagi rose to fame in Nikkatsu Action movies portraying seamen, hitmen and other macho types.

Also, though he was achingly intense on screen, Akagi was no disciple of the Method, searching, Dean-like, for a character's agonised core. Instead, he was a natural, confident of his ability to hold the screen. His quick smile, punkish nonchalance and air of loneliness were compulsively watchable, especially to his female fans. At the same time, he felt no need to impose his personality on his co-stars – he was often the most focused listener, the most spontaneous reactor. He played versions of himself in film after film, but never became mannered or stale.

In other words, he was less an actor than a star – the biggest, after Yujiro Ishihara and Akira Kobayashi, at Nikkatsu. In a career spanning barely two years, he appeared in twenty four films, and at the time of his death, his career trajectory was upward.

His nickname, "Tony," came from his perceived resemblance to the young Tony Curtis: he had the same chiselled features, pouting lips, lean, rugged build and head of tousled black hair.

Born Chikahiro Akatsuka on 8 May, 1939 in Tokyo, he had a fairly typical upbringing for the times. After evacuating to the Shonan Coast, southwest of Tokyo, to avoid wartime bombing, his family settled in nearby Hayama. He tried and failed to join the merchant marines, then entered Seijo University in Tokyo's Setagaya Ward.

In August 1958, in his freshman year, Akagi passed Nikkatsu's fourth New Faces audition. In his first film, Ko Nakahira's *Crimson Wings* (*Kurenai no Tsubasa*, 1959), he was just a face in the crowd. His real debut was in Tokujiro Yamazaki's *Pistol 0* (*Kenju no 0-go*, 1959), playing a small role as one of the many handlers of a pistol lost by an American tourist.

Akagi appeared in a total of twelve films in 1959, with his first starring role coming in the tenth, Seijun Suzuki's *The Naked Age* (*Suppadaka no Nenrei*), as the leader of a teen biker gang. Akagi and his pals hang out in an abandoned Quonset hut near an American base and create a miniature communistic society of share-and-share-alike, until he is tempted to grab more than his share. The film ends with Akagi plunging over a cliff on his bike – an eerie foreshadowing of his real-life death

Toward the end of the year Akagi appeared in two films opposite Yujiro Ishihara. In Akinori Matsuo's *Roughnecks from Shimizu* (*Shimizu no Abarenbo*) he played the delinquent son of a drug-addict father whom Ishihara's radio producer tries to save –

above: Keiichiro Akagi in "Tales of a Gunman: Quick-Draw Ryu" (Kenju Buraicho: Nukiuchi no Ryu, 1960).
opposite: Publicity shot for Keiichiro "Tony" Akagi.

but who later commits suicide. In Yoichi Ushihara's *Gambling Den Wind* (*Tekkaba no Kaze*) he portrayed a gangster rival to Ishihara's just-out-of-prison ex-con – and held his own against the studio's biggest star.

Between these two films Akagi starred in Takumi Furukawa's *College Roughnecks* (*Daigaku no Abarenbo*) as a judo-trained bouncer for a gang-run club. His true breakthrough, however, came the following year, with the four entries of the hit *Tales of a Gunman* (*Kenju Buraicho*, 1960) series. Akagi was also elevated to membership in Nikkatsu's Diamond Line, an elite group of four male stars – Yujiro Ishihara, Akira Kobayashi, Koji Wada and Akagi – who headlined the studio's action product.

He made thirteen Diamond Line films in all, not including the one he was shooting at the time of his death, *The Man Who Lives in the Torrent* (*Gekiryu ni Ikiru Otoko*). The best remembered, however, are the *Tales of a Gunman* films, in which Akagi and Joe Shishido played rival guns-for-hire who end up on the same side. They had their comic moments, with Shishido as a too-cool-for-school smoothy supplying the laughs, but their dominant tone was noirish, with Akagi saying goodbye to his love interest in the last reel.

The first, *Tales of a Gunman: Quick-Draw Ryu* (*Kenju Buraicho: Nukiuchi no Ryu*), set the pattern, as well as solidifying Akagi's star status. He plays Ryuji, a gunman who is quicker on the draw than his targets, but nicks them instead of killing them. At the

No Borders, No Limits

start of the film he gets help from an unknown – and unwanted – source on a job and finishes with a dead target instead of a wounded one. Soon after he ends up drugged and in a hospital. When he gets out, a mysterious rival gunman (Shishido), takes him to an equally mysterious benefactor – a Chinese gang boss who has paid his hospital bill and wants to employ him because he likes "first-class things." Against his will Ryuji is drawn back into the world of the gangs – and a dangerous drug deal. Along the way he meets Midori (Ruriko Asaoka), a fashion model who seems to know more than she should, but turns out to have more in common with him than he had first imagined. They are drawn closer together, though at the end they have to part.

Akagi's last film, Ushihara's *Crimson Pistol* (*Kurenai no Kenju*, 1961), was also one of his best. Unlike the many Nikkatsu Action films that bear little or no relationship to any known reality, but give no sign of that fact, *Crimson Pistol* begins with a close-up of the lantern-jawed Goro Tarumi laconically telling a client that "professional hitmen don't exist in Japan." Tarumi, we learn, was once a hitman himself, but injured his shooting arm. He has since set himself up as freelance trainer of hired killers. He finds his first student, Akagi, in a nightclub, saving a hostess (Mari Shiraki) from hoodlums who have come to reclaim her for their boss.

Akagi proves an apt pupil, with quick reflexes and the right attitude. Then he is hired by a boss fighting a drug turf war with two other gangs. His first assignment: the hostess, who knows too much about an approaching drug deal. Akagi frees her instead, placing his own life in jeopardy. The ensuing action is non-stop – and Akagi once again displays not only his talent for action, but also his essential nice guyness.

On 14 February, 1961, shortly after the successful release of *Crimson Pistol*, Akagi was driving a go-cart on the Nikkatsu lot when he lost control and slammed into a steel door. On 21 February, despite frantic efforts to save his life, he died of a brain haemorrhage. He was twenty one years old. One week before his death he recorded a song about "going once to that world beyond." Nikkatsu released it, but reshot the film he was making at the time of his accident, with Hideki Takahashi playing Akagi's role. No one, however, could take his place and Nikkatsu never recovered from his loss.

Keiichiro Akagi Selected Filmography

Crimson Wings (*Kurenai no Tsubasa*, 1959)
Pistol 0 (*Kenju no 0-go*, 1959)
The Naked Age (*Suppadaka no Nenrei*, 1959)
Roughnecks from Shimizu (*Shimizu no Abarenbo*, 1959)
College Roughnecks (*Daigaku no Abarenbo*, 1959)
Gambling Den Wind (*Tekkaba no Kaze*, 1960)
Tales of a Gunman: Quick-Draw Ryu (*Kenju Buraicho: Nukiuchi no Ryu*, 1960)
Crimson Pistol (*Kurenai no Kenju*, 1961)

Original theatrical poster for "Tales of a Gunman: Quick-Draw Ryu" (Kenju Buraicho: Nukiuchi no Ryu, 1960).

Tetsuya Watari.

Tetsuya Watari (1941-)

Handicapped by illness and unfortunate timing, but a magnetic presence on the screen and an actor of unusual skills, Tetsuya Watari was born in 1941 on Awaji Island, Hyogo Prefecture. His younger brother was actor Tsunehiko Watase. After completing his secondary education at a boarding school, Watari entered the elite Aoyama University in Tokyo. On graduating he took a test to be a Japan Airlines pilot, but failed. In 1964 he went to Nikkatsu for a New Faces contest and was scouted by a publicist while eating lunch in the cafeteria. He joined the studio, not bothering with a formal audition.

Less than six months after being signed, Watari made his screen debut in Isao Kosugi's *Wild Kishido* (*Abare Kishido*, 1965), playing Joe Shishido's younger brother. The brothers, both auto racers, join forces to get revenge after their detective father is killed by gangsters.

Watari starred in two films in his first year with Nikkatsu and played supporting roles in five more – a fast start for a newcomer. His first starring role was in Kosugi's *Judgment of Youth* (*Seishun no Sabaki*, 1965), playing a student who uses his karate skills to help his gang boss father battle a rival gang.

With his boyish good looks, long legs and fiery intensity, Watari was tagged from the start as the second coming of 1950s idol and studio saviour Yujiro Ishihara. Unfortunately, Nikkatsu's action films were losing ground to Toei's yakuza pictures and the Japanese film industry as a whole was losing ground to television. Watari's heyday was to be little like Ishihara's.

As though passing a baton between generations, Watari supported Ishihara in two films – Akinori Matsuo's *I'll Make You Cry* (*Nakaseru ze*, 1965) and Toshio Masuda's *Duel in the Red Valley* (*Akai Tanima no Ketto*, 1966). In the first film he played a second mate to Ishihara's first mate on a cargo ship. His dramatic fight scene with Ishihara on the deck in the driving rain impressed fans and boosted him toward stardom.

From his 1965 debut to the end of 1967, Watari appeared in a total of twenty six films, including four remakes of Ishihara hits. By genre, nineteen were contemporary action and seven were youth films. None were comedies or *ninkyo* pictures – both popular genres at the time.

Watari remade several of Ishihara hits, including *The Guy Who Started a Storm* (*Arashi o Yobu Otoko*, 1966), *Stars, Don't Weep: The Winner* (*Hoshi Yo Nagekuna: Shori No Otoko*, 1967), *A Slope in the Sun* (*Hi no Ataru Sakamichi*, 1967) and *Velvet Hustler* (*Kurenai no Nagareboshi*, 1967).

Toshio Masuda's loose remake of his own 1958 hit *Red Quay* (*Akai Hatoba*), with added inspiration from Godard's *Breathless*, *Velvet Hustler* was Watari's

above: Tetsuya Watari performs the yakuza rite of atonement in "Gangster VIP" (Burai Yori Daikanbu, 1968).
opposite: Chieko Matsubara and Tetsuya Watari in "Tokyo Drifter" (Tokyo Nagaremono, 1966).

personal favourite among his Nikkatsu films. He plays a happy-go-lucky hitman who, in the opening sequence, steals a red sports car, shoots a gang boss in another car on a Tokyo expressway and, whistling a tune, speeds away. Soon after, he goes to Kobe to lay low while the heat cools. A year later, he is living the easy life with a pretty bar hostess, while bossing a small gang of *chinpira*. Then trouble arrives in the form of a hitman (Joe Shishido) sent from Tokyo to whack him. Further complications arise when a local detective (Tatsuya Fuji) tags Watari as responsible for the Tokyo hit and a spoiled rich girl (Ruriko Asaoka) arrives in town to track down her missing jewel dealer fiancée. Watari ends up helping her – and trying to bed her.

Watari's true breakthrough role was as the lone-wolf gangster hero in the six films of the *Hoodlum* (*Burai*, 1968-1969) series, based on the best-selling memoirs of real-life hood Goro Fujita. Director Toshio Masuda called the first film in the series, *Gangster VIP* (*Burai Yori Daikanbu*, 1968) "a youth film that happens to be set in the yakuza world." In tone and style, however, it resembles *Street Mobster* (*Gendai Yakuza: Hitokiri Yota*), the seminal 1971 Kinji Fukasaku film that launched Bunta

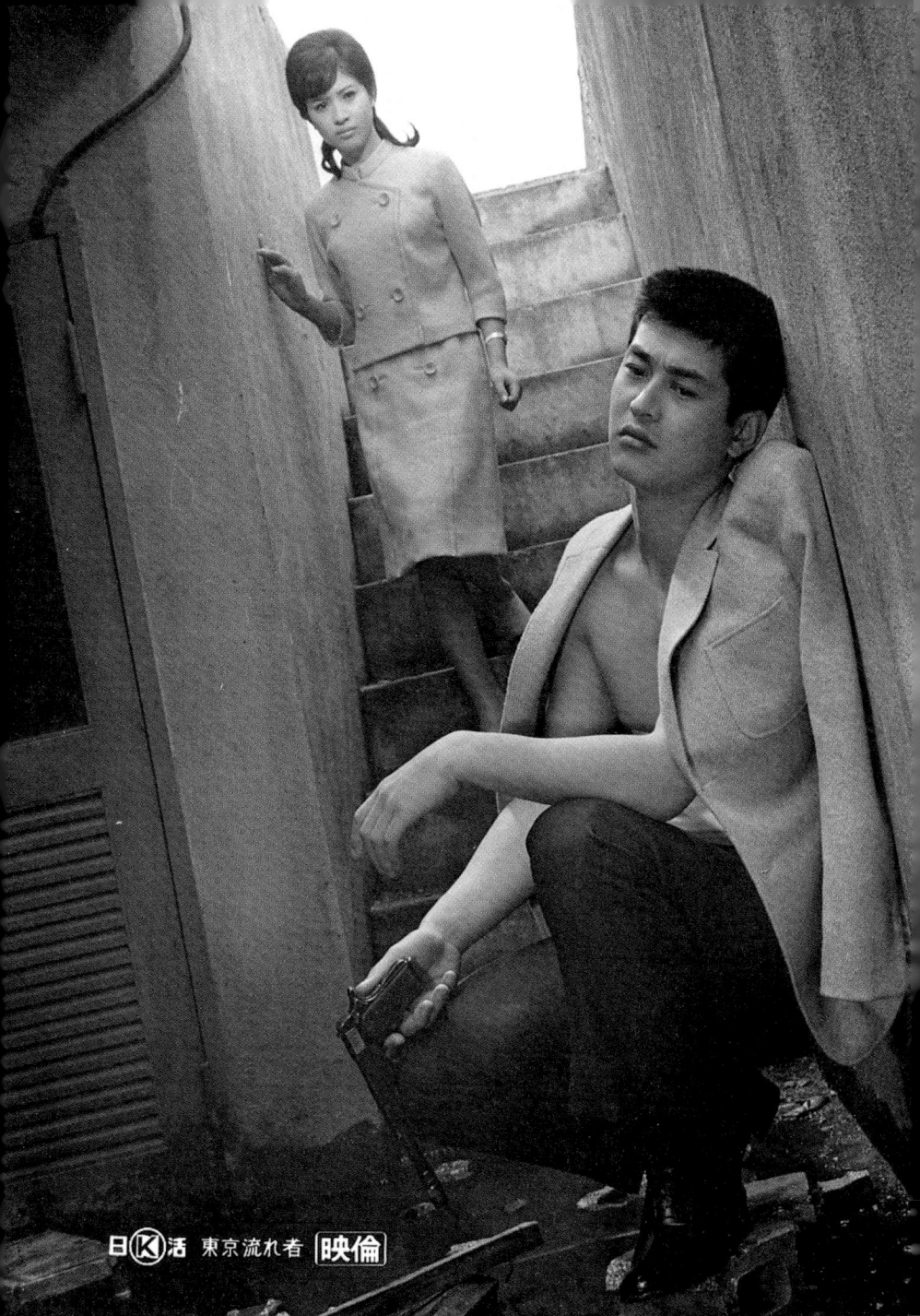

日K活　東京流れ者　映倫

Sugawara to stardom, while laying the groundwork for the more realistic Toei gangster films of the early 1970s.

Watari plays Goro, a gangster sent to prison for three years for stabbing the hitman (Kyosuke Machida) of a rival gang, the Aokis. On his release, he finds his gang in decline and learns that the hitman is still alive, but on the outs with his own gang, the Mizushimas. Goro soon finds himself in a similar situation when his gang, to head off a war with the Aokis, agrees to cut Goro loose. Friends since childhood, Goro and the hitman realise they are now brothers in exile and agree to forget the past. They also both decide to leave the yakuza life, together with the women they love. They then plot their escape from Tokyo, but tragedy intervenes – and Goro goes out to get revenge. The ending, however, is the not standard triumph of gangster right over wrong. Instead it underlines one stark truth: for Goro there is no easy way out of the world that formed him.

Watari's best-known Nikkatsu film abroad, however, is *Tokyo Drifter* (*Tokyo Nagaremono*, 1966), Seijun Suzuki's Dadaesque genre send-up. Watari plays a gangster who defends his gone-straight former boss against the machinations of murderous rivals. Forced to live on the run, he becomes involved in increasingly bizarre situations, including a barroom brawl straight out of a Hollywood Western. Watari refuses to be distracted by the film's absurdities, playing the harassed hero with his trademark intensity and cool.

In 1971 Watari left Nikkatsu and joined Ishihara Production – Yujiro Ishihara's production company. While continuing his film career, he played the title role in the NHK TV series *Katsu Kaishu*, but fell seriously ill and left the show in the middle of the season. After a year of recuperation, Watari made his screen comeback playing an out-of-control yakuza in Kinji Fukasaku's *Graveyard of Honour* (*Jingi No Hakaba*, 1975). His sensational performance, highlighted by a scene in which he chews his dead lover's bones in front of his startled boss, earned him a secure place in the genre pantheon.

After appearing in Fukasaku's *Yakuza Graveyard* (*Yakuza no Hakaba: Kuchinashi no Hana*, 1976), Watari left films for television, starring in the long-running cop shows *Big City* (*Daitokai*) and *Seibu Police* (*Seibu Keisatsu*). In the 1990s, Watari made a comeback to the big screen, with starring roles in Takao Okawara's thriller *Abduction* (*Yukai*, 1997) and Yukio Fukamachi's romantic drama *Nagasaki Strolling Song* (*Nagasaki Bura Bura Bushi*, 2000), playing opposite fellow Nikkatsu star Sayuri Yoshinaga.

In 2004 Watari starred in Hideyuki Hirayama's *Lady Joker* as the elderly leader of a kidnapping gang who wants revenge for a decades-old wrong. Though no longer the hot-eyed punk kid of old, Watari commands attention with that still strong presence, that still smoky voice that hints of fires within – and a loneliness no woman can cure.

Tetsuya Watari Selected Filmography

Wild Kishido (*Abare Kishido*, 1965)
Judgement of Youth (*Seishun no Sabaki*, 1965)
I'll Make You Cry (*Nakaseru ze*, 1965)
Duel in the Red Valley (*Akai Tanima no Ketto*, 1966)
Red Glass (*Akai Gurasu*, 1966)
The Guy Who Started a Storm (*Arashi o Yobu Otoko*, 1966)
Tokyo Drifter (*Tokyo Nagaremono*, 1966)
A Record of Love and Death (*Ai to Shi no Kiroku*, 1966)
Stars, Don't Weep: The Winner (*Hoshi yo Nagekuna: Shori no Otoko*, 1967)
A Slope in the Sun (*Hi no Ataru Sakamichi*, 1967)
Velvet Hustler (*Kurenai no Nagareboshi*, 1967)
Gangster VIP (*Burai Yori Daikanbu*, 1968)
The Blazing Continent (*Moeru Tairiku*, 1968)
East China Sea (*Higashi Shinakai*, 1968)
Whose Chair? (*Dare no Isu?*, 1968)
Big Boss (*Dai Kanbu*, 1968)
Yakuza Wanderer: Bad Guys' Work (*Yakuza Wataridori: Akuto Kagyo*, 1969)
Yakuza Unlisted: Wipeout (*Yakuza Bangaichi: Massatsu*, 1969)
Savage Wolf Pack (*Yaju o Kese*, 1969)
Showdown at Nagasaki (*Showa Yakuza Keizu: Nagasaki no Kao*, 1969)
Exiled to Hell (*Jigoku no Hamonjo*, 1969)
Outlaw: Rub-out! (*Burai Barase!*, 1969)
Ruthless Gambler (*Bakuto Mujo*, 1969)
The Cleanup (*Arashi no Yushatachi*, 1969)
Profile of a Gangster (*Yakuza Yokogao*, 1970)
Shinjuku Outlaw: Kick Out the Jams (*Shinjuku Outlaw: Buttobase*, 1970)
Goodbye Rules (*Saraba Okite*, 1971)
A Man's World (*Otoko no Sekai*, 1971)
Cockroach Cop (*Gokiburi Deka*, 1973)
The Human Revolution (*Ningen Kakumei*, 1973)
The Cockroach (*Gokiburi*, 1973)
Stray Dog (*Nora Inu*, 1973)
Theatre of Life (*Jinsei Gekijo*, 1973)
Graveyard of Honour (*Jingi no Hakaba*, 1975)
Conflagration (*Tokyo-wan Enjo*, 1975)
Human Revolution 2 (*Zoku Ningen Kakumei*, 1976)
Yakuza Graveyard (*Yakuza no Hakaba: Kuchinashi no Hana*, 1976)
Blue Christmas (1978)
The Clock: Goodbye to Winter (*Tokei: Adieu l'Hiver*, 1986)
The Milkway Railroad of the Heart: The Miyazawa Kenji Story (*Waga Kokoro no Ginga Tetsudo: Miyazawa Kenji Monogatari*, 1996)
Abduction (*Yukai*, 1997)
Diary of Early Winter Shower (*Shigure no Ki*, 1998)
Nagasaki Strolling Song (*Nagasaki Bura Bura Bushi*, 2000)
Brother (2000)
Lady Joker (2004)

Original theatrical poster for Koreyoshi Kurahara's "I Am Waiting" (Ore wa Matteru ze, 1957).

THE WOMEN OF NIKKATSU:
KITAHARA, ASAOKA, ASHIKAWA and KAJI

Mie Kitahara (1933-)

An actress whose tall, boyish figure, full-lipped, dusky beauty and coolly cosmopolitan screen persona made her a perfect match for frequent co-star Yujiro Ishihara, Mie Kitahara was born Makiko Arai in Tokyo in 1933. In 1949, after graduating from junior high school, she joined the Nishigeki Dancing Team (NDT) and in 1951 appeared in an NDT chorus line in the Toho film *Evening of Sorrow* (*Aishu no Yoru*). In 1952, she passed the Shochiku New Face audition and left NDT. That November she made her proper film debut in Keisuke Kinoshita's *Carmen Falls in Love* (*Carmen no Junjo su*), playing a young woman with a child who is abandoned by the child's father – an impecunious artist played by Rentaro Mikuni.

She acquitted herself well and Kinoshita, seeing her potential, had her adopt the professional name Mie Kitahara. She was cast in a succession of minor parts, finally attracting attention for her portrayal of an Ainu girl in the second instalment of the mega-hit film trilogy *What Is Your Name?* (*Kimi no Na wa*, 1953). Her roles, however, did not get bigger and in 1954 she left Shochiku for Nikkatsu.

Soon after arriving, Kitahara was given a leading role in Masahisa Sunohara's *The Woman's Building* (*Nyonin no Kan*, 1954). In 1955, she became one of the studio's leading female stars, working in a variety of genres with top studio directors like Kinuyo Tanaka, Yuzo Kawashima, Katsumi Nishikawa, Masahiro Makino, Kozaburo Yoshimura, Kon Ichikawa and Tomu Uchida. Her work pace was so brutal that, on the set of Makino's period drama *Tales of Jirocho's Chivalry: The Crow of Amagi* (*Jirocho Yukyoden Amagigarasu*, 1955) she burned her face and damaged her eyes from over-exposure to the arclights.

She soldiered on, however – and won critical praise for her roles in screen adaptations of serious literature, such as Kaneto Shindo's *Wandering Alone on the Shore* (*Ryuri no Kishi*, 1956), a drama based on a novel by Yoko Ota about a woman (Kitahara) who marries a doctor (Rentaro Mikuni), not knowing that he is a brutal egoist who cast aside his previous wife and child.

That May, Yujiro Ishihara made his debut in *Season of the Sun* (*Taiyo no Kisetsu*), the film that launched the Sun Tribe boom. Soon after Kitahara was cast opposite Ishihara in Ko Nakahira's *Crazed Fruit* (*Kurutta Kajitsu*, 1956), playing a girl that a callous, jaded Sun Tribesman (Ishihara) and his naive younger brother (Masahiko Tsugawa) both fall for, while she is leading a double life as a middle-aged

Yujio Ishihara and Mie Kitahara in "Red Quay" (Akai Hatoba, 1958).

American's wife. The film was a huge, influential hit that turned Kitahara – previously seen as a serious, quiet type – into a sexy Sun Tribe star.

She appeared in a spate of Sun Tribe films after that, including Takumi Furukawa's *Backlight* (*Gyakukosen*, 1956) and Ko Nakahira's *Summer Storm* (*Natsu no Arashi*, 1956), playing women who use and discard men – a turnabout from the abused women of her earlier films. The following year she again appeared with Ishihara, in Umetsugu Inoue's *The Winner* (*Shorisha*, 1957). The film, in which Ishihara plays a punk-turned-boxer, and Kitahara a ballerina he becomes involved with, was a box office smash. She also impressed in Toshio Masuda's *Red Quay* (*Akai Hatoba*, 1958), playing a pure-hearted but feisty girl who falls for Ishihara's impudent gangster. After these and other early successes Kitahara and Ishihara were paired in film after film, a total of twenty four by the time Kitahara retired in 1960.

All were hits, the biggest being Tomotaka Tasaka's family drama *A Slope in the Sun* (*Hi no Ataru Sakamichi*, 1958), in which Ishihara plays the straight-talking son of his wealthy father's mistress, Kitahara, a home tutor who is at first shocked by his frankness but, like everyone in this unusual family, falls under his spell. She also impressed in Koreyoshi Kurahara's *I Am Waiting* (*Ore wa Matteru ze*, 1957), playing a club hostess who tries to commit suicide to escape from her vicious gangster boss – and starts to find a new life with Ishihara's big-hearted restaurant manager. Their slowly blossoming star-crossed romance is touched with a brooding melancholy that is the essence of Nikkatsu noir.

Kitahara fell under her co-star's spell in real life as well. With the media rumour mill buzzing about the exact state of their relationship, Ishihara and Kitahara flew to Hawaii in January 1960 minus a wedding licence – a scandalous adventure that started a media feeding frenzy, though the couple formalised their engagement in April and married in December. Kitahara then retired from the screen. Her last film and her 24th with Ishihara, *Man at the Bullfight* (*Togyu ni Kakeru Otoko*, 1960), was released for the 1961 New Year's season – and became yet another hit.

Nikkatsu was planning one more "retirement commemoration" film to cash in yet again on the couple's popularity, but Ishihara broke a leg skiing at the Shiga Heights resort in January and his long recovery doomed the project. Kitahara appeared occasionally on television in the years that followed, but mainly devoted herself to Ishihara and his career. After his death, on 17 July, 1987, she wrote and, in 1988, published a book of reminiscences titled *Yu-chan, I Want to Hold You* (*Yu-chan Dakishimetai*).

Mie Kitahara Selected Filmography

Evening of Sorrow (*Aishu no Yoru*, 1951)
Carmen Falls in Love (*Carmen no Junjo su*, 1952)
What Is Your Name? (*Kimi no Na wa*, 1953)
The Woman's Building (*Nyonin no Kan*, 1954)
Tales of Jirocho's Chivalry: The Crow of Amagi (*Jirocho Yukyoden Amagigarasu*, 1955)
Wandering Alone on the Shore (*Ryuri no Kishi*, 1956)
Crazed Fruit (*Kurutta Kajitsu*, 1956)
Backlight (*Gyakukosen*, 1956)
Summer Storm (*Natsu no Arashi*, 1956)
The Winner (*Shorisha*, 1957)
I Am Waiting (*Ore wa Matteru ze*, 1957)
A Slope in the Sun (*Hi no Ataru Sakamichi*, 1958)
Red Quay (*Akai Hatoba*, 1958)
Man at the Bullfight (*Togyu ni Kakeru Otoko*, 1960)

Original theatrical poster for Koreyoshi Kurahara's "That Despicable Guy" (*Nikui Anchikusho*, 1962).

No Borders, No Limits

Ruriko Asaoka (1940-)

Nikkatsu Action films were, almost by definition, male oriented and male dominated. The female lead was usually the hero's love interest, not his equal or better. Yet one actress not only rose to stardom in the genre, but also transcended it, to become a generational icon for million of fans, both male and female.

Just as Nikkatsu Action films were borderless – set in ports, cities or wide open spaces where the traditional was giving way to the internationalised new (or was absent altogether) – Ruriko Asaoka's on-screen image was slightly exotic, excitingly modern. With her slim, petite figure, she may not have been a Hollywood glamour queen, but her big eyes, small face, full lips and slender, perfectly proportioned legs made her an Audrey Hepburn-like stand-out, as well as a good match for such similarly "un-Japanese" (*Nihonjin-banare*) male leads as Yujiro Ishihara and Keiichiro Akagi.

Ruriko was usually impeccably dressed, coifed and made-up even when her male love interests were playing gangsters, construction workers, starving artists or other déclassé types. She could also get down and dirty, though, as when she played a grease-smudged factory girl in *Red Handkerchief* (*Akai Handkerchief*, 1964) or when she zoomed down dusty highways in an open sports car in pursuit of lover Ishihara in *That Despicable Guy* (*Nikui Anchikusho*, 1962) And though she did her share of weeping and waiting while her hero was off slaying dragons (or punching out gangsters), she could also be flip, sassy or toweringly angry with him, in ways that looked daringly modern to her more conservative contemporaries.

Born Nobuko Muto in Xinxing, Manchuria in 1940, she moved together with her family to Tokyo after the war. In 1955 she successfully auditioned for the lead in a Nikkatsu musical, *The Distant Forest* (*Midori Haruka ni*) and made her screen debut at the age of fifteen.

Not long after, she quit school to pursue her film career, moving steadily up the Nikkatsu ladder. She was paired with Yujiro Ishihara in *The Eagle and the Hawk* (*Washi to Taka*, 1957) and *Tomorrow Is Tomorrow's Wind* (*Ashita wa Ashita no Kaze*, 1958), while starring in the *Wanderer* and *Drifter* series with Akira Kobayashi and in the *Tales of a Gunman* series with Keiichiro Akagi. These roles made her famous – by the early 1960s her face was appearing on magazine covers with metronomic regularly – but she was still more of a star than an actress. (She was also romantically linked by the tabloids to Kobayashi, until he married pop signer singer Hibari Misora in 1961.)

Then, working with Koreyoshi Kurahara, she made *Ginza Love Story* (*Ginza no Koi no Monogatari*, 1962), *That Despicable Guy* (*Nikui Anchikusho*, 1962) and *Running Fever* (*Shuen*, 1964) – films that stretched her acting talents beyond what was required in most of her Nikkatsu films.

above: Ruriko Asaoka with fellow Nikkatsu star Akira Kobayashi.
opposite: Keiichiro Akagi and Ruriko Asaoka in "Tales of a Gunman: Quick-Draw Ryu" (Kenju Buraicho: Nukiuchi no Ryu, 1960).

In *Ginza Love Story* she played an aspiring fashion designer who loses her memory after a near-fatal traffic accident. In *That Despicable Guy* she was the bossy, teasing manager/lover of a popular TV and radio personality (Ishihara), who nearly loses him when he leaves her, his job and his entire life for a self-imposed mission of charity. In *Running Fever* she portrayed a new bride who has to bear up alone after her husband is torn away from her by the war. Ruriko gave a passionate, committed performance considered a career peak.

After the Nikkatsu Action boom faded in the middle of the decade she soldiered on – and did some of her best work, including her part as the sassy, spoiled rich girl searching for her missing (and unregretted) jewellery dealer fiancée in *Velvet Hustler* (*Kurenai no Nagareboshi*, 1967).

That year Ruriko left Nikkatsu to pursue a freelance career. In 1969 she co-starred with Ishihara in the action adventure *Safari 5000* (*Eiko e no 5,000 Kilo*) – the last time they would be paired on screen.

Her marriage shortly after to fellow actor Koji Ishizaka did not end her career. Instead, she kept working throughout the 1980s, including four well-remembered

appearances as the "Madonna" (i.e. love interest) in Yoji Yamada's *Tora-san* series about a wandering peddler, played by Kiyoshi Atsumi, who is forever falling in love but never gets the girl.

From the 1980s Ruriko's screen roles became fewer, but she continued to make frequent stage and television appearances. In 2000 she separated from Ishizaka and in 2004 was romantically linked with Makoto Matsui, a stage actor two decades her junior, with whom she had made a duet record.

Ruriko Asaoka Selected Filmography

The Eagle and the Hawk (*Washi to Taka*, 1957)
Tomorrow Is Tomorrow's Wind (*Ashita wa Ashita no Kaze*, 1958)
Guitar Wanderer (*Guitar o Motta Wataridori*, 1959)
Tales of a Gunman: Quick-Draw Ryu (*Kenju Buraicho: Nukiuchi no Ryu*, 1960)
Ginza Love Story (*Ginza no Koi no Monogatari*, 1962)
That Despicable Guy (*Nikui Anchikusho*, 1962)
Running Fever (*Shuen*, 1964)
Velvet Hustler (*Kurenai no Nagareboshi*, 1967)
Safari 5000 (*Eiko e no 5,000 Kilo*, 1969)
Goyokin (1969)

Izumi Ashikawa (1935-)

An idol to millions of male Nikkatsu fans, including animation-master-to-be Hayao Miyazaki, for her combination of pixieish charm and gutsy determination, Izumi Ashikawa was born Sachiko Ito in Tokyo in 1935. In 1952 she quit high school to train with SKD (Shochiku Kageki Dan), a dance troupe modelled on the Radio City Music Hall Rockettes. Taking the professional name Izumi Ashikawa, she was scouted by director Yuzo Kawashima, then still with Shochiku, at a fashion show in 1953 and cast in Kawashima's comedy *The Tokyo Madam and the Osaka Wife* (*Tokyo Madam to Osaka Fujin*, 1953).

In 1955, with Kawashima's encouragement, Ashikawa left SKD and Shochiku for Nikkatsu. That year she made her first film for the studio, Kon Ichikawa's *Ghost Story of Youth* (*Seishun Kaidan*), playing a girl enamoured of Mie Kitahara's androgynous ballerina. Over the next two years, she and Kitahara emerged as the studio's brightest young female stars, with Ashikawa appearing in everything from romantic dramas and melodramas to period films and comedies.

In 1956, she was cast with Yujiro Ishihara in Tomotaka Tasaka's *The Baby Carriage* (*Ubaguruma*), playing an innocent girl confronted by her father's mistress and the baby they have had together. Further complications ensue when the mistress's cheerfully insolent younger brother (Ishihara) arrives on the scene – and Ashikawa finds herself attracted to him.

The Baby Carriage's box office success freed Ishihara from his punkish Sun Tribe image and boosted Ashikawa to stardom. After that, she starred with Ishihara in film after film, including such action dramas as Ko Nakahira's *Crimson Wings* (*Kurenai no Tsubasa*, 1959), Yoichi Ushiyama's *If You're a Man, You Gotta Dream* (*Otoko nara Yume o Miro*, 1959) and Toshio Masuda's *The Brawler* (*Kenka Taro*, 1960). She also played second lead to Mie Kitahara and Ishihara in such films as *The Guy Who Started a Storm* (*Arashi o Yobu Otoko*, 1957), *A Slope in the Sun* (*Hi no Ataru Sakamichi*, 1958) and *Roughnecks from Shimizu* (*Shimizu no Abarenbo*, 1959).

As these roles indicate, Ashikawa was similar to Hideaki Nitani in the Nikkatsu Action hierarchy – not quite a star of the first rank, but not just a supporting player either. She lacked Kitahara's cool sensuality and Ruriko Asaoka's stylish, cosmopolitan flair, which made her a runner-up in the Nikkatsu Action Queen competition. However, she projected a purity, crossed with spunkiness and vulnerability, that made her an idol for the more high-minded, traditional or shy sort of Japanese guy, who wanted to worship and protect his inamorata, not be intimidated by her.

Following Kitahara's retirement in 1961, Ashikawa starred in more films with Ishihara, including *He and I* (*Aitsu to Watashi*, 1961), *A Bold Life* (*Dodotaru Jinsei*, 1961)

Izumi Ashikawa gets a taste of Joe Shishido in "Glass Johnny: Look Like a Beast"
(Glass no Johnny: Yaju no yo ni Miete, 1962).

日活 野獣のように見えて

and *The Arab Storm* (*Arab no Arashi*, 1961). She was also paired with other young Nikkatsu male stars in a variety of genres, including Ryoji Hayama in *The Beauty* (*Kajin*, 1958), Akira Kobayashi in *The Perfect Game* (*Kanzen na Yugi*, 1958), Tamio Kawachi in *The Beginning of Knowledge and Love* (*Chi to Ai no Shuppatsu*, 1958) and Hiroyuki Nagato in *Break Down That Wall* (*Sono Kabe o Kudake*, 1959).

Ashikawa broke with her good girl image playing the simple-hearted, cruelly victimised prostitute in Koreyoshi Kurahara's *Glass Johnny: Look Like a Beast* (*Glass no Johnny: Yaju no yo ni Miete*, 1962), a drama based on Fellini's *La strada*. Her performance was a career highlight. After this triumph, Ashikawa continued to be cast in youth films, playing older sister types to younger actresses like Sayuri Yoshinaga and Masako Ota (Meiko Kaji), while appearing with Hideki Takahashi in the *ninkyo* film *Tales of Japanese Chivalry: Invitation to a Bloodbath* (*Nihon Ninkyoden Chimatsuri Kenkajo*, 1966) and Tetsuya Watari in the 1966 remake of the 1957 Yujiro Ishihara hit *The Guy Who Started a Storm* (*Arashi o Yobu Otoko*).

After being romantically linked with Ryoji Hayama, her co-star in several romantic dramas, Ashikawa married Nikkatsu young hopeful Tatsuya Fuji in August 1968 and, after appearing in Kenji Yoshida's *Sun of the Archipelago* (*Retto no Taiyo*, 1968), retired from films.

Izumi Ashikawa Selected Filmography

The Tokyo Madam and the Osaka Wife (*Tokyo Madam to Osaka Fujin*, 1953)
Ghost Story of Youth (*Seishun Kaidan*, 1955)
The Baby Carriage (*Ubaguruma*, 1956)
Crimson Wings (*Kurenai no Tsubasa*, 1959)
If You're a Man, You Gotta Dream (*Otoko nara Yume o Miro*, 1959)
The Brawler (*Kenka Taro*, 1960)
The Guy Who Started a Storm (*Arashi o Yobu Otoko*, 1957)
A Slope in the Sun (*Hi no Ataru Sakamichi*, 1958)
Roughnecks from Shimizu (*Shimizu no Abarenbo*, 1959)
He and I (*Aitsu to Watashi*, 1961)
A Bold Life (*Dodotaru Jinsei*, 1961)
The Arab Storm (*Arab no Arashi*, 1961)
The Perfect Game (*Kanzen na Yugi*, 1958)
The Beauty (*Kajin*, 1958)
The Perfect Game (*Kanzen na Yugi*, 1958)
The Beginning of Knowledge and Love (*Chi to Ai no Shuppatsu*, 1958)
Break Down That Wall (*Sono Kabe o Kudake*, 1959)
Glass Johnny: Look Like a Beast (*Glass no Johnny: Yaju no yo ni Miete*, 1962)
Tales of Japanese Chivalry: Invitation to a Bloodbath (*Nihon Ninkyoden Chimatsuri Kenkajo*, 1966)
The Guy Who Started a Storm (*Arashi o Yobu Otoko*, 1966)
Sun of the Archipelago (*Retto no Taiyo*, 1968)

Meiko Kaji (1947-)

After serving a long apprenticeship miscast in minor "good girl" roles, Meiko Kaji emerged in the late 1960s as the mini-skirted queen of the New Action genre, her combination of icy cool, smouldering looks and kick-ass toughness marking her as utterly unlike a previous generation of more traditionally feminine Nikkatsu leading ladies. Born Masako Ota in Tokyo in 1947, she was scouted by Nikkatsu in 1965, while working as an assistant for MC Keizo Takahashi and playing for her high school basketball team. Entering the studio under her real name, she made her screen debut in Katsumi Nishikawa's *Sad Song of Parting* (*Kanashiki Wakare no Uta*, 1965).

She was then cast in a quick succession of youth movies opposite stars Hiroyuki Ota and Mitsuo Hamada, but her strong on-screen personality didn't fit the genre's sweet ingenue mould and she found all but bit parts hard to come by for the next three years. In 1969 she was cast in the all-star *ninkyo* film *Remnants of Japanese Chivalry* (*Nihon Zankyoden*) and, at the request of director Masahiro Makino, changed her professional name to Meiko Kaji.

The new name not only gave her a new image ("Kaji" means "oar" or "shaft" – more the name for a yakuza tough guy than a kimonoed maiden), but also a boost toward stardom. She was cast as a woman warrior in Yasuharu Hasebe's *Code of the Red-Light District* (*Moriba Jingi*, 1969) and Teruo Ishii's *The Blind Woman's Curse* (*Kaidan Noboriryu*, 1970). That year, she also starred in Hasebe's *Woman Boss: Stray Cat Rock* (*Onna Bancho: Nora Neko Rock*, 1970) – the first instalment of a five-part series, as a girl gangbanger who is the fighting equal of any of her male punk acquaintances. In the second instalment, *Wild Jumbo* (1970), Kaji demonstrated a husky-voiced singing talent that she was to parlay into a lucrative second career.

Kaji also played less caricatured, more realistically lonely rebels in Yukihiro Sawada's *Melody of Rebellion* (*Hangyaku Melody*, 1970) and Toshiya Fujita's *Shinjuku Outlaw: Kick Out the Jams!* (*Shinjuku Outlaw Buttobase!*, 1970). Before she could properly expand her range or build on her early stardom, however, the Nikkatsu New Action boom faded. In August 1971 the studio stopped production, only to restart in November with a new line of soft porn films. After appearing in seventy films in seven years, Kaji left the studio. Her first stop was Toei, which was looking to replace Junko Fuji, a pillar of the studio's *ninkyo* genre, who had retired in March 1972 to marry a Kabuki actor.

Among the films Kaji made for Toei, some of the best known abroad belong to the *Female Convict Scorpion* (*Joshu Sasori*) series, starting with Shunya Ito's *Female Prisoner #701: Scorpion* (*Joshu 701-go Sasori*, 1972) – a garish, leering exploitation

Meiko Kaji (above) and the gang in "Stray Cat Rock: Sex Hunter" (Nora Neko Rock: Sex Hunter, 1970).

pic about women in prison, based on a popular comic. Despite all the porny shenanigans, Kaji remains a glowering, powerful figure. There were six instalments altogether, the last released in 1977, but Kaji starred in only the first four. Her rendition of the theme song of the fourth instalment, Hasebe's *Female Prisoner Scorpion #701: Grudge Song (Joshu 701-go Uramibushi*, 1973), sold 1.2 million copies for Decca Records.

In 1973 she left Toei to go freelance, though she still continued to appear in Toei films. That year, she starred in another manga adaptation – Toshiya Fujita's *Lady Snowblood (Shurayukihime*), a period drama about a woman (Kaji), born in prison, who takes bloody revenge on the killers of her father. Quentin Tarantino's referencing of the film, including its four-chapter plot structure, in the *Kill Bill* films, as well as his use of two Kaji *enka* numbers on the soundtrack of *Kill Bill: Vol. 1*, raised Kaji's international profile. The film was also a hit in Japan, though the sequel, Fujita's *Lady Snowblood: Love Song of Vengeance (Shurayukihime Urami Renga*, 1974) was less successful.

In 1976, she starred in Kinji Fukasaku's *Yakuza Graveyard (Yakuza no Hakaba: Kuchinashi no Hana)* as a troubled woman of mixed Korean and Japanese ancestry. Since then Kaji has worked only sporadically in films, instead concentrating on television, with many appearances in mysteries and dramas. One unusual non-action role, as a prostitute who commits suicide with her lover in Yasuzo Masumura's *Double Suicide of Sonezaki (Sonezaki Shinju*, 1978), won her several domestic Best Actress awards.

Meiko Kaji Selected Filmography

Sad Song of Parting (Kanashiki Wakare no Uta, 1965)
Remnants of Japanese Chivalry (Nihon Zankyoden, 1969)
Code of the Red-Light District (Moriba Jingi, 1969)
The Blind Woman's Curse (Kaidan Noboriryu, 1970)
Woman Boss: Stray Cat Rock (Onna Bancho: Nora Neko Rock, 1970)
Stray Cat Rock: Wild Jumbo (Nora Neko Rock: Wild Jumbo, 1970)
Stray Cat Rock: Sex Hunter (Nora Neko Rock: Sex Hunter, 1970)
Melody of Rebellion (Hangyaku Melody, 1970)
Shinjuku Outlaw: Kick Out the Jams! (Shinjuku Outlaw Buttobase!, 1970)
Female Prisoner #701: Scorpion (Joshu 701-go Sasori, 1972)
Female Prisoner Scorpion #701: Grudge Song (Joshu 701-go Uramibushi, 1973)
Lady Snowblood (Shurayukihime, 1973)
Lady Snowblood: Love Song of Vengeance (Shurayukihime Urami Renga, 1974)
Yakuza Graveyard (Yakuza no Hakabe Kuchinashi no Hana, 1976)
Double Suicide of Sonezaki (Sonezaki Shinju, 1978)

THE BEST OF THE REST:
SHISHIDO, NITANI, KANEKO, KAWACHI, TAKAHASHI and FUJI

Joe Shishido (1933-)

Best known in the West as the rice-gobbling hitman in Seijun Suzuki's *Branded to Kill* (*Koroshi no Rakuin*, 1967), Joe Shishido became a Nikkatsu star by portraying characters who often begin as hitmen, conmen and other disreputable types, but end up on the side of the hero, if not always the angels. Also, in an era when contemporary action stars were mostly latter-day samurai – the epitome being the stoic gangsters played by Ken Takakura – Shishido was a glaring exception, a smoothy who dressed too loud and talked too fast, with an insolent grin or leer on his chipmunk-cheeked face.

He was not just showing off and stealing scenes – though he did both with abandon – but also injecting verve and humour into what would have otherwise been bland genre fare. His performances often verged on self parody, but he usually kept them from going over the line.

Tall and lanky in the mould of studio mega-star Yujiro Ishihara, Shishido could handle a gun or his fists with skill and panache. In other words, he was capable of playing the tough-guy hero as well the colourful sidekick. His rise to the top was something of a fluke, but once he arrived, he showed he belonged.

Shishido was born in 1933 in Osaka's Kita Ward, the third of four sons and one daughter. His younger brother later became the actor Eiji Go. He attended schools in Tokyo and Miyagi Prefecture and, after graduating from high school in 1952, entered the theatre course of Nihon University's Arts Department. In March 1954 he successfully auditioned for Nikkatsu's New Face contest – one of 21 who passed, out of 8,000 applicants. Dropping out of college, he entered Nikkatsu and began appearing in bit roles.

He made his screen debut under his own name in Seiji Hisamatsu's *Policeman's Diary* (*Keisatsu Nikki*, 1955), as a young patrolman who takes on a police chief (Masao Mishima) in a kendo bout. Noting that a Shishido was a villain in the popular novel *Miyamoto Musashi*, studio bosses asked him to change his name – they envisioned him as a romantic lead, not a bad guy – but he refused.

In 1957, unhappy with his blandly handsome features, Shishido underwent plastic surgery to flesh out his cheeks, giving him a more ruggedly masculine look. Soon after he started getting larger parts, mainly as dodgy, disreputable characters in action films. He got a boost to stardom playing Akira Kobayashi's rival in the hit

above: Joe Shishido *(left)* and Jerry Fujio *(behind)* in the hide-out in "A Colt Is My Passport" (Colt wa Ore no Passport, 1967).
opposite: Hideaki Nitani *(left)* and Joe Shishido *(right)* plot a scam in "Dirty Work" (Rokudenashi Kagyo, 1961).

Wanderer (*Wataridori*) series. He portrayed similar characters in Kobayashi's *Drifter* (*Nagaremono*) series and Keiichiro Akagi's *Tales of a Gunman* (*Kenju Buraicho*) series, both also money-earners for Nikkatsu. Given the nickname "Ace no Joe" (Ace Joe), he rose to national popularity. In December 1960 he became the fifth member of Nikkatsu's New Diamond Line of top male action stars.

Following Ishihara's skiing accident in January 1961 and Akagi's death in a go-cart crash a month later, Shishido and veteran second lead Hideaki Nitani were asked to take up the slack, beginning with Shishido's first starring role in Buichi Saito's *Dirty Work* (*Rokudenashi Kagyo*, 1961), a comic buddy film co-starring Nitani.

They play two scuffling freelance hoods who brawl with a gang of stevedores – and catch the eye of local shipping company boss (Nobuo Kaneko). He hires them to blow up a hulk for the insurance money, which they do with naughty glee. They take their earnings from this job to a gambling den where Shishido wins – and Nitani whips out a pistol. He steals the entire pot and skips out, leaving his erstwhile pal behind.

Soon after, Nitani goes to the insurance company to find out who was behind the scam, with a scam of his own in mind. Meanwhile, Shishido starts to work as muscle for

the boss. These two meet again, as they must, this time as battling scam artists. The resulting comedy of false identity stops just short of farce, with both heroes finally joining the side of good, though for how long no one knows.

Shishido also starred in Takashi Nomura's Eastern Western *Fast-Draw Guy* (*Hayauchi Yaro*, 1961), playing Ace Joe, a bounty hunter in the wide open spaces of Northern Japan, who arrives in a small town with a captive slung over his horse – a robber who stole the payroll for the construction crew at a nearby dam. Joe claims the reward, but the town fathers are suspicious of this cocky stranger. A local saloon girl, Jane (Yoko Minamida), falls for him, but she and the other girls are under the thumb of the slithery saloon boss (Nobuo Kaneko). Joe decides to stand up to the boss and the rest of his gang, with the aid of the plucky but green young sheriff. The ensuing action is based on Anthony Mann's *The Tin Star* (1957), with Shishido playing the Henry Fonda role. The execution, however, borders on parody, with Shishido, as usual, supplying most of the laughs.

From his promotion to stardom in March 1961 to the end of the year Shishido appeared in eleven films, including *Bodyguard Work* (*Yojimbo Kagyo*) and *Helper Work* (*Suketto Kagyo*), the latter starring Hiroyuki Nagato as Shishido's rival/ally in place of Nitani. These sequels failed to hold fans' attention, however, and the *Work* series died a premature death.

Ishihara and Kobayashi had been able to sustain a similarly blistering production pace, but they had star images and winning formulas already in place, which made it easier for the studio to maintain quality, like an assembly plant working from a good blueprint. Shishido's producers, however, had to make it up on the fly, more like factory workers designing their own machinery while turning out product. No wonder some of the gears failed to mesh.

In 1962 Shishido kept making program pictures, including the borderless action films that had become a Nikkatsu trademark. Among his most unusual films from this period was Koreyoshi Kurahara's *Glass Johnny: Look Like a Beast* (*Glass no Johnny: Yaju no yo ni Miete*, 1962). Inspired by Fellini's *La strada* and filmed in black-and-white, *Glass Johnny* fits into none of the standard Nikkatsu categories and has few of the standard Nikkatsu touches.

Shishido plays a bike track tout who tries to manage a losing cyclist to success when he encounters a prostitute (Izumi Ashikawa) on the run from her brothel and the pimp (Ai George) who works for it. The prostitute is pure-hearted, weak-minded, apparently helpless. The tout nobly protects her from the pimp – as long it is convenient. When it is not, he discards her – and the pimp grabs her. Then the pimp is stabbed on a train platform and taken into custody by the police – and the prostitute then nurses him back to health. Neither of the men, we see, deserve her, though both finally want her. Much as Anthony Quinn did for Fellini, Joe subsumes his larger-than-life persona into Kurahara's vision and turns in a surprisingly moving performance.

He gave his comic side full rein again in Ko Nakahira's caper film *Danger Paws* (*Yabai Koto Nara Zeni ni Naru*, 1962), playing a gangster who hears about the theft of a truck full of the paper used for printing money and has the bright idea of kidnapping an engraver and partnering with the robbers to make counterfeit notes. Two other hoods (Hiroyuki Nagato and Kojiro Kusanagi) have the same brainstorm, however. After several twists and turns, including Shishido's bruising encounter with a female judo expert (Ruriko Asaoka), these three join forces, but the road to riches is not a smooth one.

By the end of 1962, Shishido had starred in twenty one films. From 1963 to 1967, he starred in twenty three more, but played twenty three supporting roles as well. Ten of these forty six films were, like the *Work* series, comic actioners, twenty five hard-boiled action, and ten *ninkyo* action. One, Seijun Suzuki's *Gate of Flesh* (*Nikutai no Mon*, 1964), fell into its own category, with Shishido playing a cynical ex-soldier who becomes the pet and protector of a gang of whores in early post-war Japan.

In Suzuki's *Youth of the Beast* (*Yaju no Seishun*, 1963), Shishido honed his tough-guy image, albeit with comic flourishes. He played a disgraced ex-cop who infiltrates two yakuza gangs in an attempt to clear both his name and that of a superior who was found dead in a double suicide with a call girl. Shishido brought his usual combination of impudence and energy to the role, while remaining oblivious, on screen at least, to Suzuki's parodistic shenanigans.

Shishido also worked with Suzuki on *Detective Bureau 2-3: Go to Hell, Bastards* (*Tantei Jimusho 2-3 Kutabare Akuto-domo*, 1963), a comic caper film that, with its touches of surrealist style and absurdist humour, was a hint of excesses to come.

Shishido's best-known role internationally is that of Goro Hamada in Suzuki's *Branded to Kill* (*Koroshi no Rakuin*, 1967). Famous as the film that got Suzuki fired from Nikkatsu, *Branded to Kill* also did little for Shishido's career at the time. Despite his full-bore performance as Hamada, who is struggling to rise in the hitman hierarchy when a botched job for a half-Japanese, half-Indian femme fatale thrusts him into a nightmarish struggle for survival, the film tanked at the box office. Shishido later reminisced about going to see it with friends – and finding almost no one else in the theatre.

He showed his hard-boiled side in Yasuharu Hasebe's *Slaughter Gun* (*Minagoroshi no Kenju*, 1967), playing one of three brothers (the other two are Tatsuya Fuji and Jiro Okazaki), who live on the wrong side of the law. After Shishido's night club manager is forced by his boss to murder a woman, he quits his gang – and ends up fighting a life-or-death battle with its members, including an old friend and romantic rival (Hideaki Nitani), who has become a deadly enemy.

Another action highlight from this period is Takashi Nomura's *A Colt Is My Passport* (*Colt wa Ore no Passport*, 1967). Shishido plays a hitman hired by a gang to whack a rival oyabun (gang boss). He does the deed with a sniper rifle and, together with a nervous sidekick (Jerry Fujio), makes his escape. Their troubles, however, are just beginning – before they can board their getaway plane they are snatched by thugs from the rival gang. Through Shishido's quick thinking, they make a narrow escape and flee to a cheap inn for truckers near Yokohama. They arrange for passage on a boat, but while they are driving to the dock in a truck... enough to say that they miss their ride, while the enemy closes in.

The climactic shoot-out, staged on a lonely beach with several mind-bending, breath-taking stunts, may strain credibility, but Shishido's panache and cool are on full display. The film remains one of his favourites.

In the late 1960s, Nikkatsu's entire action lineup began to fall from favour and Shishido found roles harder to come by. He appeared in the films of other studios, while shifting the focus of his activities to television.

During this period, he also starred in New Action films, including *Yakuza Wanderer: Bad Guys' Work* (*Yakuza Wataridori: Akuto Kagyo*, 1969), an all-star vehicle for Shishido, Akira Kobayashi and Tetsuya Watari that recycled *Work* series tropes, and *Bloody Battle* (*Ryuketsu no Koso*, 1971), playing an ex-con who goes on a mission of revenge after his gang is crushed by a larger rival.

Joe Shishido in "Red Gun Belt" (Kurenai no Gun Belt, 1961).

In 1971, for the first time in eighteen years, Shishido found himself without a studio contract. He appeared in Toei's *jitsuroku* ("true story") gang films, including Kinji Fukasaku's *Battles Without Honour and Humanity: The Final Episode* (*Jingi Naki Tatakai Kanketsuhen*, 1974), as an out-of-control gang boss.

When yakuza movies began to fall from auidience favour in the mid-1970s, Shishido put his hard-boiled persona into storage. Over the next two decades, he worked primarily as a TV personality, while making occasional forays into films, including Nobuhiko Obayashi's *Transfer Students* (*Tenkosei*, 1982), *Bound for the Fields, the Mountains and the Seacoast* (*Noyuki Yamayuki Umibeyuki*, 1986) and *A Mature Woman* (*Onna Zakari*, 1994).

In the 1990s, Shishido returned to his tough guy past, playing a gruff detective mentor to Masatoshi Nagase's scruffy PI in Kaizo Hayashi's *The Most Terrible Time in My Life* (*Waga Jinsei Saiaku no Toki*, 1994), *Stairway to the Distant Past* (*Haruka na Jidai no Kaidan o*, 1994) and *The Trap* (*Wana*, 1996). He also occasionally appeared in straight-to-video yakuza movies, including the intriguingly titled *Gangster Jihad: Holy War* (*Gokudo Jihad: Seisen*, 2002). In 2005 he played an impotent art connoisseur who loses his sexually frustrated wife to a drunken-but-passionate artist in Takashi Ishii's S&M drama *Flower and Snake 2* (*Hana to Hebi 2*).

Joe Shishido Selected Filmography

Policeman's Diary (*Keisatsu Nikki*, 1955)
Woman of the Ginza (*Ginza no Onna*, 1955)
Mother (*Ofukuro*, 1955)
The Maid's Kid (*Jochukko*, 1955)
The Crimes of Kamisaka Shiro (*Kamisaka Shiro no Hanzai*, 1956)
Rusty Knife (*Sabita Knife*, 1958)
Voice Without a Shadow (*Kagenaki Koe*, 1958)
The Spring That Didn't Come (*Fumihazushita Haru*, 1958)
Guitar Wanderer (*Guitar o Motta Wataridori*, 1959)
Plains Wanderer (*Daisogen no Wataridori*, 1960)
Tales of a Gunman: Quick-Draw Ryu (*Kenju Buraicho: Nukiuchi no Ryu*, 1960)
The Man with the Fearless Laugh (*Kenju Burai-cho: Futeki ni Warau Otoko*, 1960)
The Sun Bearer (*Taiheiyo no Katsugiya*, 1961)
Dirty Work (*Rokudenashi Kagyo*, 1961)
Fast-Draw Guy (*Hayauchi Yaro*, 1961)
Bodyguard Work (*Yojimbo Kagyo*, 1961)
Helper Work (*Suketto Kagyo*, 1961)
Red Gun Belt (*Kurenai no Gun Belt*, 1961)
Mexican Vagabond (*Mexico Mushuku*, 1962)
Glass Johnny: Look Like a Beast (*Glass no Johnny: Yaju no yo ni Miete*, 1962)
Danger Paws (*Yabai Koto Nara Zeni ni Naru*, 1962)
Detective Bureau 2-3: Go to Hell, Bastards (*Tantei Jimusho 2-3 Kutabare Akuto-domo*, 1963)

Youth of the Beast (*Yaju no Seishun*, 1963)
Theatre of Life (*Jinsei Gekijo*, 1964)
Gate of Flesh (*Nikutai no Mon*, 1964)
Gambler's Code (*Otoko no Monsho: Ryuko Mujo*, 1966)
Asiapol Secret Service (*Asia Himitsu Keisatsu*, 1966)
A Colt Is My Passport (*Colt wa Ore no Passport*, 1967)
Branded to Kill (*Koroshi no Rakuin*, 1967)
Slaughter Gun (*Minagoroshi no Kenju*, 1967)
The Dirty Seven (*Shichinin no Yaju: Chi no Sengen*, 1967)
Retaliation (*Shima wa Moratta*, 1968)
Roughneck (*Arakure*, 1969)
Yakuza Wanderer: Bad Guys' Work (*Yakuza Wataridori: Akuto Kagyo*, 1969)
The Desperate Outlaw (*Sutemi no Narazumono*, 1970)
Comedy of Youth: The Shameless School (*Seishun Kigeki: Harenchi Gakuen*, 1970)
The Shameless School: The One About the Physical Exam (*Harenchi Gakuen: Shintai Kensa no Maki*, 1970)
The Shameless School: The One About the Tackle Kiss (*Harenchi Gakuen: Tackle Kiss no Maki*, 1970)
The New Shameless School (*Shin Harenchi Gakuen*, 1971)
Wet Highway (*Furyo Shojo Mako*, 1971)
Bloody Battle (*Ryuketsu no Koso*, 1971)
New Hoodlum Soldier: The Line of Fire (*Shin Heitai Yakuza: Kasen*, 1972)
Battles Without Honour and Humanity: The Final Episode (*Jingi Naki Tatakai Kanketsuhen*, 1974)
The Japanese Way of Chivalry: Smash (*Nihon Ninkyodo: Gekitotsuhen*, 1975)
Conflagration (*Tokyowan Enjo*, 1975)
Dead Horizon (*Genkai Nada*, 1976)
The Alaska Story (*Alaska Monogatari*, 1977)
Honour and Humanity: and War (*Jingi to Koso*, 1977)
The Eye's Visitor (*Hitomi no Naka no Homonsha*, 1977)
A Tale of Sorrow and Sadness (*Hishu Monogatari*, 1977)
Bandits Vs. Samurai Squad (*Kumokiri Nizaemon*, 1978)
Edo Porn (*Hokusai Manga*, 1981)
Transfer Students (*Tenkosei*, 1982)
Our Wedding (*Oretchi no Wedding*, 1983)
Carib: Symphony of Love (*Carib: Ai no Symphony*, 1985)
Bound for the Fields, the Mountains and the Seacoast (*Noyuki Yamayuki Umibeyuki*, 1986)
Don't Mess with My Woman (*Boku no Onna ni Te o Dasuna*, 1986)
The Samurai (1987)
You Will Come to Love Me (*Kimi wa Boku o Suki ni Naru*, 1989)
Nozomi (Heart) Witches (*Nozomi (hato) uicchiizu*) (1990)
The Setting Sun (*Rakuyo*, 1992)
The Victors (*Shorishatachi*, 1992)
8 Man (*Eitoman: Subete no Sabishii Yoru no tame ni*, 1992)
A Mature Woman (*Onna Zakari*, 1994)
The Most Terrible Time in My Life (*Waga Jinsei Saiaku no Toki*, 1994)
Stairway to the Distant Past (*Haruka na Jidai no Kaidan o*, 1994)
The Trap (*Wana*, 1996)
To Love (*Aisuru*, 1997)
Drowning Fish (*Oboreru Sakana*, 2000)
Gangster Jihad: Holy War (*Gokudo Jihad: Seisen*, 2002)
Flower and Snake 2 (*Hana to Hebi 2*, 2005)

No Borders, No Limits

An interview with Joe Shishido
by Mark Schilling and Mamiko Kawamoto

Q: How did you happen to join Nikkatsu? You were still in college at the time.

Shishido: In my second year of college. I was in the theatre course of Nihon University's Arts Department.

Q: Did you want to be an actor from the beginning?

Shishido: I wanted to be a movie star. But I thought I could learn acting if I went into the theatre course. I could get a pretty good idea of what acting was before taking the film course.

Q: When you joined Nikkatsu you had a lot of competition.

Shishido: That was the first time for Nikkatsu to recruit new people – 1954. They had 8,000 apply. They picked twenty one – that's a one-in-forty ratio. I was the top one.

At first I played the third biggest role after the star, in about seven films. I thought I was something hot. I kept strange hours, I lost weight, I was living with a woman. But I was about ten years ahead of myself – I had to sweat a little bit. [laughs] By that I mean I didn't get any work for about three months. I thought maybe I ought to quit and go somewhere else, but I wanted Japanese people to know the name Joe Shishido. It didn't matter what, I would do it: the fourth lead in a gang movie, the third lead as a salaryman. I did about two or three pictures like that.

TV broadcasting started in Japan in 1953. On 1 February NHK started broadcasting, then on 28 August, NTV. Back then the studios had what they called the "five company agreement." Shochiku, Toho, Daiei, Toei and Shin Toho were angry at Nikkatsu for trying to make films, so if anyone went to Nikkatsu, the other five studios wouldn't use them. They couldn't even go on television. But we newcomers were not subject to the five company agreement, so we could appear on TV. Even if we were doing only bit parts in films, we could get big roles on television. I got the lead role in *Botchan* and other dramas – that gave me a lot of confidence. About that time, Nikkatsu said that I shouldn't be doing so much TV.

Then all six [major film] companies joined forces to boycott television. I asked the studio how I could sell myself. What was I supposed to do? They said "Something will turn up." I said "What is 'something'? Give me an example." They threatened me, saying "If you don't do as we say, you'll be on television all right – only television."

Q: You tried to get an edge by having an operation on your cheeks. You were pretty skinny then – did you do it because you wanted to look bigger, more macho?

Shishido: No, I wanted to look handsomer – that's what plastic surgery is all about. Every day at the studio they told me an actor shouldn't be skinny. I knew it – they didn't have to keep harping on about it. Then I made the discovery of the century – full cheeks. [laughs] I had them inject me to fill out my cheeks.

Q: So that was your idea?

Shishido: Right, my idea. Then my cheeks started to cave in a bit, so I had them inject me again to fill them out some more, like Orson Welles. [laughs]

Q: You liked Orson Welles?

Shishido: Yes, I liked him. I played hitmen – my nickname was "Hitman Joe." I played that role in *Quick-Draw Ryu* (*Nukiuchi no Ryu*) in the *Tales of a Gunman* (*Kenju Buraicho*) series. Also in Akira Kobayashi's *Wanderer* (*Wataridori*) series and the *Drifter* (*Nagaremono*) series. When I appeared with Yujiro Ishihara it was always as a bad guy, but I only made five or six films with him.

Q: Always a bad guy?

Shishido: With Yujiro, yes, always a bad guy. With the others there was more of a humorous side to my characters. I was a hitman who could get laughs.

*Q: Watching **Quick-Draw Ryu**, I was impressed by not only the gags and so forth, but also by your costumes. You put together a total look. [laughs] Was that your own idea?*

Shishido: You means the spats and all that? Yes, I came up with a lot of the costumes myself.

Q: It's hard to think of anyone in Hollywood quite like you. You were something unique.

Shishido: I can't say I was unique. One guy who gave me ideas then was Henry Silva. Another was Orson Welles. Body movement I imitated from Burt Lancaster. When I was doing action scenes I tried to remember how he did them. Twirling the pistol I got from Kirk Douglas in *Man Without a Star*. I stole nearly everything from Hollywood. [laughs] I just snapped it up. I think it's amazing now, the way I crammed things into my head. And that hyena laugh of Richard Widmark – hee, hee, hee. I picked that up right away.

I started watching Hollywood movies from the age of four. The first one I saw was *King Kong*. Before the war American movies were flooding into Japan. After the Manchurian Incident we were at war with China, fighting against Chiang Kai-shek and the Nationalist Army. Even then foreign movies were coming in. Then after Pearl Harbor and the start of the Pacific War, foreign films in English were prohibited. On 15 August, 1945 Japan lost the war. The first American film to arrive after that, in September, was John Wayne's *Tall in the Saddle*. I used to listen to FEN, the Far East Network radio – *Buttons and Bows* [starts singing]. I heard that song when I was a first year student in junior high. When I was twelve Bob Hope and Bing Crosby movies came to Japan. Then Jane Russell's. But the one that really influenced me was James Cagney in *The Oklahoma Kid*. That's how I ended up this way. [laughs]

Q: When I saw you in **Fast-Draw Guy** (**Hayauchi Yaro**)*, I was thinking of Jack Palance. Maybe it was the black clothes. [laughs]*

Shishido: No, that costume was what Burt Lancaster wore in *Vera Cruz*. In *Shane* Jack Palance put on his glove and told Elisha Cook Jr. to draw. Cook drew but Palance already had his pistol in his hand and shot him. When Palance appeared George Stevens had the thunder crash.

I got a lot of ideas from not only American movies, but Italian movies as well, including Pietro Germi's. When I was in college I watched Italian and French films. Alain Delon is French isn't he? *Plein soleil*. I liked Gérard Philipe. And Fernandel, the Italian comedian. *Il ferroviere*. *La strada* by Federico Fellini. *Glass Johnny* (*Glass no Johnny: Yaju no yo ni Miete*) is based on *La strada*.

Q: That film was a departure for Nikkatsu, wasn't it?

Shishido: We all tried to figure out how Fellini had gotten that atmosphere. We didn't want to just make a copy, but we wanted to look good by comparison. That's why we wanted to know how he had done it.

The first film I starred in, *Dirty Work* (*Rokudenashi Kagyo*, 1961), was based on Humphrey Bogart and Edward G. Robinson's *Key Largo*. They take out an insurance policy on a hulk, blow it up and get the money. We ripped off that part and turned it into a comedy.

What I really wanted to do, though, was something like a Roaring Twenties gang film. I like those black-and-white gang films set in the days of Prohibition.

Hideaki Nitani *(top)* and Joe Shishido *(bottom)* hang out in "Dirty Work" (Rokudenashi Kagyo, 1961).

*Q: What about Hollywood film noir – was that an influence as well? I get that impression from watching **Rusty Knife** (**Sabita Knife**) and films from that era.*

Shishido: Yes, that was an influence, on everyone from the director to the actors. I was the one who knew that genre best.

Q: And Toshio Masuda?

Shishido: Masuda was the best at stealing. [laughs]

Q: He was about seven or eight years older that you. How did he rank in the studio hierarchy?

Shishido: Nikkatsu started with the producer system. The producer ranked above the director. But when Yujiro Ishihara came along, they switched to the star system. They had what they called the Diamond Line: Yujiro, Akira, Keiichiro Akagi and Koji Wada, but Wada didn't appear in a lot of films. They had me change my nickname from Hitman Joe to Ace Joe. At first they just had four guys in the Diamond Line, but then the theatre owners asked the studio to make Hitman Joe a lead actor.

Q: What about Hideaki Nitani? Wasn't he promoted as well?

Shishido: Nitani came in at the same time as Akira Kobayashi. There was another one – an actress named Hisako Tsukuba. She would strip for the camera, though her films weren't real porn. She was the one who discovered James Cameron – she was a producer on his first film, *Piranha II: Flying Killers*.

*Q: I see you've written your autobiography [points to Shishido's new book **Shishido: A Novel About Nikkatsu Studio** (**Shishido: Shosetsu Nikkatsu Satsueijo**, Shinchosha, 2004)].*

Shishido: I thought I would write it like a hard-boiled novel, but I decided to change to a more intimate style. The other, hard-boiled way was stupid – it had no nuance. The first printing was only 10,000 copies, so I told the publisher that when I wrote the next one, I wouldn't give them any rights. [laughs]

   I'm thinking of writing the second volume this year. The first book goes up to when I started getting starring roles. So this time I want to write about the joy and hardship and sadness of being a star – and whether it was worth the struggle. I starred in 54 films and was in 300 altogether, including bit parts. I don't think you'll find another one like me anywhere else.

*Q: Your most recent film is **Flower and Snake 2 (Hana to Hebi 2)**.*

Shishido: I play the husband of Aya Sugimoto. I own a gallery – I'm an art critic. I can't get it up any more. [laughs] I'm seventy, she's thirty five. She's hot, but I can't satisfy her sexually. I tell this master of Nihonga (Japanese-style painting) that the most beautiful thing in life is when you're confident that you're doing something well, even something that would be boring if an ordinary guy did it. Then I take five Viagra capsules and die. [laughs]

At the end I have sex, but this body of mine is seventy years and three months old. When I get naked, I don't look it – that's the good part. But my pubic hairs are white – I have a complex about that, it makes me feel inferior. When I touch a woman's body I can't get it up. It's a movie about impotence. They even shot on location – I heard it cost a lot of money.

I have also had a DVD I made – I'll lend it to you if you like. It's called *Dirty Joker*. It's about the four different faces I've had in the course of my life, including the one I was born with. I wanted to sell myself, so I've done these dirty things to my face.

Q: How long did it take to make?

Shishido: About 500 days altogether – it's already done. It's a documentary. An actor has to be willing to do anything for a role. You have to control what's inside of you. You have to have to be able to bring out the fear, the sadness, the pain, the positive feelings, the negative feelings, the sexual impulses. That's the theme – it's something that interests me.

Q: [Watching the video] You've got some familiar faces in there – Akagi, Ishihara, Kobayashi.

Shishido: A lot of actors appear. When we had the publication party for the book a lot of them came. I'd gotten fat, so I had an operation, then went to the party. That's the easiest way to explain the story. It's about the changes I've gone through.

Q: Getting back to Nikkatsu – you used to grind out films at an incredible pace.

Shishido: The studio would release eight double bills a month, fifty two a year. Each double bill was two films, so that made 104 a year. I would star in ten or twelve.

Q: Was there ever any time for rehearsal?

Shishido: No, none. When Yujiro broke his leg and Keiichiro Akagi died, Akira Kobayashi and I were the whole star rotation. When I did *Dirty Work*, I didn't even have a script. I did for the next one, *Fast-Draw Guy*. It was a remake of a Henry Fonda movie, *The Tin Star*. After that I did *Bodyguard Work* (*Yojimbo Kagyo*, 1961), but when they started shooting I had no idea what I was supposed to do.

Q: You didn't know the story?

Shishido: At first I had three pages with just that day's lines. I was told to memorise them quickly. Then they shot one scene after another, bang, bang, bang. After one week they finally finished the script. [Mimes looking at the script.] So this is what it's about! What kind of crap is this? [laughs] They kept doing it that way for about a year. That year I starred in twelve films and played supporting roles in two more.

Q: With Yujiro Ishihara out of commission and Keiichiro Akagi gone did you feel any pressure as the new studio star? Did you worry what might happen if you couldn't hack it?

Shishido: I didn't worry about what might happen – I was where I was and I just had to get on with it. I couldn't let the studio go bust. Yujiro would be out for nearly nine months, so I had to keep things going until he came back. Then they brought Nitani up. Then along came Hideki Takahashi. They had a plan to bring up Akira Nakao, but it didn't work out. What really kept the studio afloat then were the romantic dramas with Sayuri Yoshinaga and Mitsuo Hamada. Hideki Takahashi did his bit as well, but the studio lost out to television. The audience gradually got smaller and smaller.

*Q: About that time you made **Fast-Draw Guy**. It was something like a Spaghetti Western.*

Shishido: It came along three years before the Spaghetti Westerns. It was a Miso Western. [laughs]

*Q: It was also a buddy movie, but it came out a long time before **Butch Cassidy and the Sundance Kid** (1969), which is considered the first Hollywood buddy movie.*

Shishido: Well, there were the Bing Crosby and Bob Hope movies, but those were comedies.

Joe Shishido in shades in "Branded to Kill"
(Koroshi no Rakuin, 1967).

Q: Takahashi was mainly used in period gang pictures – but it seemed that you were cast mostly in contemporary films. Was that your own preference?

Shishido: No, I also appeared in samurai dramas. I was in seven NHK maxi-dramas (*taiga dorama*). When I first joined Nikkatsu I appeared in a lot of period films. But the samurai I played were pretty stupid types. [laughs]

*Q: That was the Golden Age of the samurai films – with Akira Kurosawa getting a lot attention abroad for **The Seven Samurai (Shichinin no Samurai**, 1954) and so on. Did any of that have an impact on you?*

Shishido: Akira Kurosawa was great. His first film was a judo picture, *Sugata Sanshiro*, in 1943. I thought that film was great, then he got the Venice Grand Prix for *Rashomon* (1950). That was based on a Ryunosuke Akutagawa story, *In a Grove* (*Yabu no Naka*). When Kurosawa shot a film, he'd spend all day on one scene. If he didn't like what he saw, he'd have everyone rehearse.

Back then Toshiro Mifune would drink until he was blotto. Then he'd get his hunting rifle and when a dog started barking at night he'd yell "shut up" and – pow! He was amazing. In the later part of his career – after *Yojimbo* (1961) – he changed. He wasn't his old self any more.

Q: Kurosawa was with Toho then – they gave him the money and the time to make the kind of films he wanted. But Nikkatsu was more like a conveyor belt.

Shishido: That's what it was – a conveyor belt. You had to make sure you put the label on right. Some like Shohei Imamura put it on a little crooked. And then there were the ones who got caught in the conveyor belt, like Seijun Suzuki.

Q: You made a lot of films with Suzuki. How did he differ from the other Nikkatsu directors?

Shishido: When that guy made a movie he wouldn't sleep. He'd come every morning at nine o'clock and work until ten at night. Then, he'd go back, drink Suntory Daruma whiskey and think about what he was going to do tomorrow. Then morning would come and he'd say "I want to shoot it like this, but how can I do it?"

For example, in *Gate of Flesh* (*Nikutai no Mon*, 1964) Yumiko Nogawa is a prostitute who experiences the joy of being a woman for the first time. Suzuki had this scene in mind: When I spread her thighs, a crossfire opens up. Yumiko Nogawa's hand grabs at the air. When I touch her breast, a spray of female come hits the screen. Then when we have intercourse, a spray of male come hits the screen. When she climaxes, she feels the joy of being a woman for the first time. He wanted to do it all in one cut, with the camera moving 180 degrees. The question was how to do it. How do you do the female come? The audience might get it confused with the male come. [laughs]

He went outside the studio, put two pieces of glass in front of the lens and, using castor oil, made clear female come. Now for the semi-circular movement. [Gestures a camera movement] You squirt the come and then you do this. [Gestures a camera movement.] Then you squirt the male come. [Imitating Suzuki] "OK, We got it." When he sees the rushes, he realises he's made a perfect semi-circle. "OK everyone, that's great. You did a wonderful job." That's how we made *Gate of Flesh*.

Q: You couldn't make real porno back then, at least in the big studios, but Suzuki told me that film was as close as you could come.

Shishido: There were five remakes of *Gate of Flesh*. The first was like a porno film, but they gradually became better. I was in the second remake.

*Q: His most popular film abroad, though, is **Branded to Kill (Koroshi no Rakuin).***

Shishido: That was a great movie – for something incomprehensible. Suzuki brought in a cartoon drawing and said "This is a sex scene, but I don't want to make it smutty – I want to shoot it like this cartoon." We shot at the fountain in front of the National Stadium. We shot Annu Mari coming out of the shower – she's a butterfly collector. The story's about how these hitmen decide their ranking. But when this one hitmen smells rice in a rice cooker, he gets a hard on. We thought up some strange stuff for that one.

Q: So it wasn't Suzuki's brain child alone?

Shishido: No, Suzuki was the director, but the writers were Hachiro Guryu and his apprentices. Atsushi Yamatoya was one. Of all of them, including [Nikkatsu President] Kyusaku Hori, maybe one is still alive. Hori liked movies, but he couldn't understand that one and fired Suzuki. The story is all over the place. *Gate of Flesh* won awards at film festivals in France and elsewhere. *Branded to Kill* got a few as well. People over there thought it was interesting. A few Japanese understood it, like the members of the Waseda University film study circle. It was popular with them, but no one came to see it. I mean no one.

Jerry Fujio *(left)* and Joe Shishido *(right)* encounter Chitose Kobayashi's angel of the truck stop in "A Colt Is My Passport" (Colt wo Ore no Passport, 1967).

Q: That's my favourite Suzuki film.

Shishido: I like *Gate of Flesh*. Some people prefer *Youth of the Beast* (*Yaju no Seishun*, 1963). I'm the actor who's appeared in the most Seijun Suzuki movies. *Voice Without a Shadow* (*Kagenaki Koe*, 1958), *The Spring That Didn't Come* (*Fumihazushita Haru*, 1958). I just had bit parts in those. Then there was *Detective Bureau 2-3: Go to Hell, Bastards* (*Tantei Jimusho 2-3 Kutabare Akuto-domo*, 1963), *Youth of the Beast* (*Yaju no Seishun*), *Gate of Flesh* (*Nikutai no Mon*), *Branded to Kill* (*Koroshi no Rakuin*). I even appeared in his comeback picture *A Tale of Sorrow and Sadness* (*Hishu Monogatari*, 1977). He's made a new one recently.

*Q: **Princess Raccoon** (**Operetta Tanuki Goten**, 2005).*

Shishido: I've heard it isn't any good. Young people today don't know how to be good assistant directors. They aren't educated properly. They're just standing around staring off into space. Even if you explain they don't understand. So what do you do? What can a director do? Just give up.

The movie companies have all gone bust. The first one to go was Shin Toho. Then Nikkatsu almost went bankrupt. Shochiku, the same. All they have now is the *Free and Easy* (*Tsuri Baka Nisshi*) series and Yoji Yamada. Toho is scraping by – it's a kind of subcontractor. Toei is making a picture here and there. Daiei is now part of Kadokawa. They're sitting around wondering what they ought to make.

Japanese directors used to start as assistant directors. After ten years, they'd get to make a movie. In that time they'd learn all sorts of things about making films. If they do this, they can make money. But it's been thirty five years since that system collapsed. Nearly forty really. No one is training the next generation. The kids are trying hard to raise money and make movies. So now you have a thirty-one-year-old kid going to Hollywood and making a hit.

Q: Takashi Shimizu, the horror director.

Shishido: He was really lucky.

*Q: Yujiro went to Hollywood as well, to make **Those Magnificent Men in Their Flying Machines** (1965).*

Shishido: That was about an 80-day airplane race. Yu-chan didn't get much out of it.

Q: Did you ever get any offers from Hollywood?

Shishido: Yeah, *The Bad News Bears Go to Japan* (1978), but Antonio Inoki got the part. I couldn't speak English very well.

Q: You went abroad too, for Koreyoshi Kurahara's **Mexican Vagabond (Mexico Mushuku**, *1962).*

Shishido: I broke my leg. I had a bad feeling [before it happened]. Then I suffered a slight fracture and had to go into the hospital.

A lot of the Nikkatsu films were shot abroad – they'd just kind of pick up and go. Ishihara made *The Arab Storm* (*Arab no Arashi*, 1961) and *Man at the Bullfight* (*Togyu ni Kakeru Otoko*, 1960) abroad. Akira Kobayashi made *The Wanderer Who Crossed the Waves (Hato o Koeru Wataridori*, 1961) – he went to Bangkok for that one. I went to Southeast Asia and Mexico. The [*Mexican Vagabond*] cast and crew went to Mexico City – it's at an elevation of about 3,000 metres. Everyone got altitude sickness.

After everyone went away to work on location, I broke my leg, but they asked me to come along anyway. Nikkatsu gave some money to this teacher at Jikei Medical School. Then they gave some money to a doctor ranked under this teacher. Then they gave some money to this doctor's student. But this doctor said "No matter how much money you give me, a broken bone takes three months to heal." Then he said, "But if he really wants to go, it's a different story." I said "No problem, I'll go."

Once I got there, I had to get to work right away – I had a lot of scenes to make up. In all my scenes I was supposed be running, but I couldn't run – I'd broken my leg. So they had me walk for the first half. Otherwise, no changes.

I felt wiped out – I had altitude sickness. I didn't know – I wondered why one can of beer could make me so drunk. It was because of the altitude. But they shot the movie so you couldn't tell. There were eight Japanese, including the actors. Then there was the local crew, of course.

Q: Koreyoshi Kurahara liked foreign locations, didn't he? Several of his films were shot abroad. His style was different from Suzuki's, though. It was more European, more Nouvelle Vague.

Shishido: He was influenced by the Nouvelle Vague – Godard, Truffaut and so on. Kurahara became a director before Suzuki, though. You're supposed to write scripts with some clear idea of what images you want, but he wouldn't do it that way. He wasn't any good at first – like his debut film with Yujiro, *I Am Waiting* (*Ore wa Matteiru ze* , 1957), but he got better later.

*Q: I also understand that you like Takashi Nomura's **A Colt Is My Passport** (**Colt wa Ore no Passport**, 1967).*

Shishido: Before that one I was just playing the bad guy to Keiichiro Akagi and Akira Kobayashi. That film was a good break for me – I had a starring role fall into my hands. When I was making *Dirty Work* I felt that my life as a star had begun. Then I got *A Colt Is My Passport* and Hasebe's *Slaughter Gun* (*Minagoroshi no Kenju*, 1967) – those were my three big leading roles. If they'd let me have leading roles from the beginning, my career as a star would have been longer. But I've been in 300 movies – 170 for Nikkatsu. I don't think anyone can beat me there.

Q: I understand that you wrote a diary while you were at Nikkatsu.

Shishido: I used it for my book. Shinchosha printed 10,000 copies, but they're gone. I'm going to write the next volume now – I've got tons of material. In another ten years or so there won't be any more real studios, so I have to describe what the studio of the 20th Century was like for those who come after. That's why I'm writing.

*Q: Akira Kobayashi recently published a book as well. [**For a Warm Heart** (**Atsuki Kokoro ni**), Futabasha, 2004]*

Shishido: That's a scam. He blabbed away and a ghostwriter wrote it up. Everything he said was just his own imagination. He's gradually succumbed to his own megalomania. You build yourself up bigger and bigger and that's what happens to you. He's about 6 billion yen ($53 million) in debt and has about 70 mortgages, but he's doesn't think it's any big deal. He says he paid them off.

Yujiro Ishihara used to get mad at him. "Who says you graduated from Meiji University – you've got no education, you idiot!" I was senior to both of them. They would call me "Joe-san" [Note: San is an honourific]. When we were together I'd call them "Yu-chan" and "Akira." [Note: Chan is a diminutive.] But in public I'd call them Yujiro Ishihara-sama and Akira Kobayashi-sama. [Note: Sama is an honourific, more polite than san.]

Q: Toshio Masuda made a lot of films with Ishihara.

Shishido: He was the top director in the studio – he made all those Yujiro Ishihara pictures. But the one who made Yujiro a star was a producer named Takiko Mizunoe. Taki-san. Then there was Umetsugu Inoue – he was probably the best. Yujiro worked

Original theatrical poster for "A Colt Is My Passport" (Colt wa Ore no Passport, 1967).

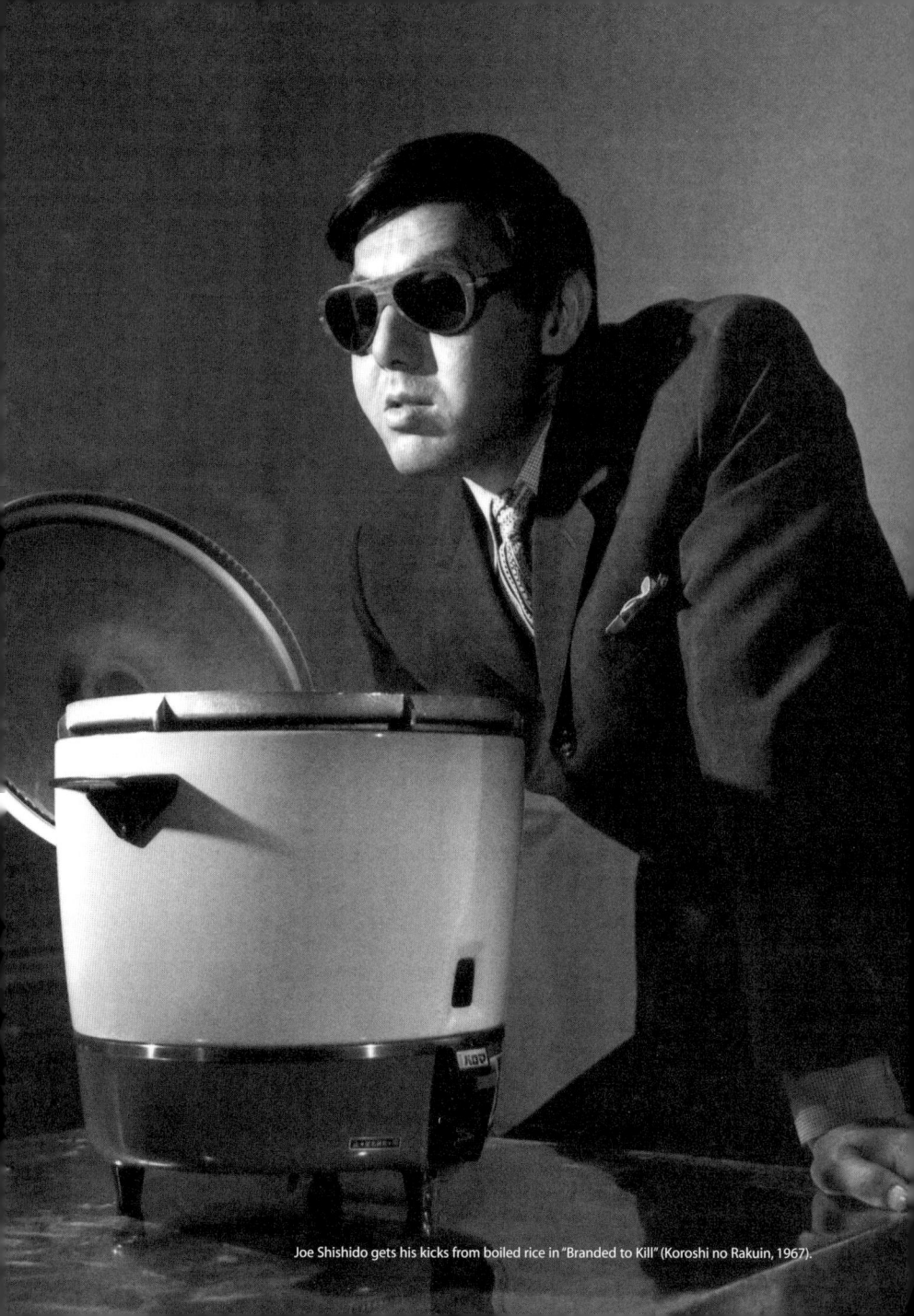

Joe Shishido gets his kicks from boiled rice in "Branded to Kill" (Koroshi no Rakuin, 1967).

with Takumi Furukawa. Then with Ko Nakahira on *Crazed Fruit* (*Kurutta Kajitsu*). His biggest hit, though, was Inoue's *The Guy Who Started a Storm* (*Arashi o Yobu Otoko*). After that they put him with Toshio Masuda.

Q: Are you friends with him?

Shishido: I wouldn't say friends. I don't feel that way about him. I like his *Red Handkerchief* (*Akai Handkerchief*) the best. There's this Nikkatsu freak – a director named Toshihiko Yahagi – who made a movie called *Again* (1984). He uses about fifteen minutes of *Red Handkerchief* in the film. The scene in the Yokohama Grand Hotel where Ruriko Asaoka is in Yujiro's room and Yujiro is hiding from her. Then the detective, Nobuo Kaneko, walks in and says "If he comes here, contact us." But he's already there.

Q: He sings in that film, as well as in a lot of others. What about you?

Shishido: I sang. Nikkatsu made me sing – I had to do it. I sang twenty seven songs, always the theme song and the interlude. I even put out records. I finally made them stop – there's nothing more embarrassing when you can't carry a tune than being forced to sing. I sang on *Fast-Draw Guy*, but it made me sick. I got the hives. [laughs]

Akira had more hit songs than Yujiro, but they both ended up making about the same money. They got about the same royalties. No one could surpass those two. Akagi had about two records. Ruriko Asaoka had about one. The same goes for Hideki Takahashi and Tetsuya Watari. After that, no one.

Q: Have you written any other books?

Shishido: Just one hardback. I wrote a cookbook too – I'll give you a copy.

Q: [Pointing to the cookbook cover photo] You look a lot different.

Shishido: That's me. I had twenty three grams here [points to cheek]. On both sides. It wasn't silicone either – it was organogen, made from gasoline. Nasty stuff.

Q: Getting back to what we talked about earlier – you said you had the injections because you were too thin, but didn't being too handsome have something to do with it? I heard that you had it done because you didn't want to be a romantic lead.

Shishido: Well, a little. In the beginning I was in nothing but these arty films...

Q: And you wanted to do action?

Shishido: Ultimately I wanted to do fight scenes. When I was growing up boys would play *chanbara* [sword-fighting] or doctor. We and the girls would show each other our sex organs and think about the difference. We also played with toy pistols or rifles. If you played those sort of games until about the age of seven, no one thought it a crime. Now they'd probably call us paedophiles. [laughs] But if you do those sorts of things when you're a kid, you don't become a criminal when you're an adult.

When we played with pistols and swords we were basically acting out movies. We'd play Zorro, ride on hobbyhorses, anything and everything. I was tall so I liked *chanbara*.

Q: You were athletic?

Shishido: I was the best – better than Yujiro and Akira. I was older than them, though. I was MVP at the company baseball game twice. Akira couldn't play baseball – he was a judoist. He was good at sumo too, but he couldn't beat me. When I was forty five I won the championship in a celebrity sumo tournament. But I can't play an instrument – just cook.

Q: The perfect husband!

Shishido: But I'm not home that much.

Q: And you like to write.

Shishido: I keep a journal – when something occurs to me I write in it. "Tokyo Tower goes well with the morning sun."

Q: I suppose you're good at horseback riding as well.

Shishido: There was no one better. The stuntmen were crap. I'm the type who really has to try everything, even dancing. When I was forty I learned to tap dance. I played a tap dancing gangster – it was at the Nissei Theatre. When they came to ask me about the part, I asked them why they thought I could tap dance. I thought it was a stunt for *Candid Camera*. Anyway, someone came to teach me at three in the morning. We ended up drinking forty three bottles of beer. Back then I could drink a sumo wrestler under the table.

Joe Shishido in 2005 – still cool with a pistol.

Hideaki Nitani (1930-)

Though briefly a member of the New Diamond Line, Hideaki Nitani was less a star than a versatile second lead, who could work both sides of the good/bad divide with authority. With the soft, handsome features of a Las Vegas pop crooner – think a young Steve Lawrence – he was perfect as the smooth, sophisticated operator, but he could also throw a punch as hard as any beetle-browed tough guy. And as he proved in his pairings with Joe Shishido, he could even play comedy, though his usual role was straight man.

Born in Kyoto on 28 January, 1930, Nitani was admitted to the English Department of Doshisha University, an elite private college in Kyoto. Dropping out in 1952, he drifted through a series of interpreting jobs until he was hired by Nagasaki Broadcasting Corporation (NBC). Assigned to Sasebo, a port town that was the site of a large US naval base, he worked for NBC as an English-language newscaster.

In June 1956 he passed the third Nikkatsu New Face audition, together with Akira Kobayashi. His first significant role was in Seijun Suzuki's *Inn of the Floating Weeds* (*Ukigusa no Yado*) the following year, playing a gangster wrongly accused of murder who sets out to find the real killer.

Over the next few years, Nitani appeared in a steady stream of starring and supporting roles, with the latter outnumbering the former. By the time he joined the New Diamond line in 1961, he had starred in fifteen films, with six being features, the rest featurettes.

One of his better remembered roles from this period was the boxer-turned-gang-boss in Koreyoshi Kurahara's *I Am Waiting* (*Ore wa Matteiru ze* , 1957), especially the climactic fight scene in which he waves off his underlings and goes mano-a-mano with Yujiro Ishihara's two-fisted hero. He also played a gangster out to kill Ishihara in Toshio Masuda's *Red Quay* (*Akai Hatoba*, 1958) and a thief who hijacks the plane Ishihara is piloting in Ko Nakahira's *Crimson Wings* (*Kurenai no Tsubasa*, 1959).

Nitani worked with other Nikkatsu stars as well, playing a gun broker whose life is saved by Akira Kobayashi – and whose brother is killed by Kobayashi's lover – in Masuda's *Yakuza Ballad* (*Yakuza no Shi*, 1960) and a research scientist who is the older brother to Keiichiro Akagi's boxer hero in *Knock Down* (1960).

It was not until 1961, in Buichi Saito's *Dirty Work* (*Rokudenashi Kagyo*, 1961), that Nitani truly hit his stride, playing opposite Joe Shishido in the first instalment of a three-part comic action series. One model was the Bob Hope and Bing Crosby *Road* series, but the action elements of the series also made it a precursor to the Hollywood buddy movies of the late 1960s and beyond. When Ishihara broke his left leg skiing in January 1961 and Akagi died after a go-cart crash in February, Nitani was elevated to the New Diamond Line group of elite male action stars. Shishido, who had joined the Line slightly earlier, acquired the nickname Ace no Joe (Ace Joe), and Nitani the ungainly moniker Dump Guy, for his supposed dump-truck-like power.

That same year Nitani starred in Akinori Matsuo's comic actioner *No-Good Guy* (*Rokudenashi Yaro*), playing a gang-fighting priest in a pseudo-Western town, the first of eight New Diamond Line films that Nitani would headline in 1961.

The following year, Nitani starred in six films and played supporting roles in three. His slip in status was signalled by his last starrer for the year, *A Colt Is the Song of a Lonely Man* (*Colt wa Samishii Otoko no Uta sa*, 1962), which was filmed in black-and-white, though New Diamond Line films were, by definition, colour. Another of his films from this period, *Shotgun Guy* (*Shotgun no*

Hideaki Nitani, one of Nikkatsu's elite New Diamond Line group of male action stars.

Otoko, 1961) was an Eastern Western, but Nitani more often played detectives in modern urban settings. He also impersonated a jazzman in *Seven Contenders* (*Shichinin no Chosensha*, 1961), a former boxing champion in *The Quiet Man of the Mean Streets* (*Ankokugai no Shizukana Otoko*, 1961) and a card and dice sharp in *Black Dice* (*Kuroi Dice*, 1962).

Original theatrical poster for "Black Dice" (Kuroi Dice, 1962).

No Borders, No Limits

In 1963 Nitani reverted to being a second lead, playing a crooked-cop-turned-businessman opposite Ishihara in Toshio Masuda's *Red Handkerchief* (*Akai Handkerchief*, 1964), with Shishido as a friend-turned-enemy in Yasuharu Hasebe's *Slaughter Gun* (*Minagoroshi no Kenju*, 1967) and as Akira Kobayashi's gangster ally in Hasebe's *Retaliation* (*Shima wa Moratta*, 1968). In the West, however, he is perhaps best known as the lone-wolf yakuza who gives Tetsuya Watari's on-the-run hero refuge in Seijun Suzuki's *Tokyo Drifter* (*Tokyo Nagaremono*, 1966).

In 1971, Nitani left Nikkatsu and did occasional film work for Toei and other companies, but devoted most of his energies to television. He also launched his own school, Rec Kyoto, where he taught acting and English.

Starting in 1977 he enjoyed a ten-year run as Police Superintendent Kiyosuke Kamishiro in the hit cop series *Special Investigations Frontline* (*Tokuso Saizensen*). He also appeared in the TV drama series *Scoop Reporter* (*Tokudane Kisha*), *Snows of Winter* (*Fuyu no Yuki*) and *The Girl Who Came in the Summer* (*Natsu ni Kita Musume*), as well as commercials for Nissan Motors, East Japan Railway Company and other companies.

His marriage to Nikkatsu actress Yumi Shirakawa produced a daughter, Yurie, who became an actress and married pop idol Hiromi Go. Their divorce in 1998 produced splashy headlines in the weeklies.

Nitani has long been involved with Japan Team of Young Human Power, an NPO that, since 1993, has built more than 100 schools in Cambodia.

Hideaki Nitani Selected Filmography

Inn of the Floating Weeds (*Ukigusa no Yado*, 1957)
I Am Waiting (*Ore wa Matteiru ze*, 1957)
Red Quay (*Akai Hatoba*, 1958)
Crimson Wings (*Kurenai no Tsubasa*, 1959)
Yakuza Ballad (*Yakuza no Shi*, 1960)
Knock Down (1960)
Dirty Work (*Rokudenashi Kagyo*, 1961)
No-Good Guy (*Rokudenashi Yaro*, 1961)
A Colt Is the Song of a Lonely Man (*Colt wa Samishii Otoko no Uta sa*, 1962)
The Man with the Hollow-Tip Bullets (*Sandanju no Otoko*, 1961)
Seven Contenders (*Shichinin no Chosensha*, 1961)
The Quiet Man of the Mean Streets (*Ankokugai no Shizukana Otoko*, 1961)
Black Dice (*Kuroi Dice*, 1962)
Red Handkerchief (*Akai Handkerchief*, 1964)
Tokyo Drifter (*Tokyo Nagaremono*, 1966)
Slaughter Gun (*Minagoroshi no Kenju*, 1967)
Retaliation (*Shima wa Moratta*, 1968)

Nobuo Kaneko (1923-1995)

The king of Nikkatsu Action character actors, who played cagey, ruthless underworld types reminiscent of Edward G. Robinison's, right down to the cigar clenched in his teeth, Nobuo Kaneko was born in Tokyo in 1923. He made his screen debut in Mikio Naruse's *The Descendants of Urashima Taro* (*Urashima Taro no Koei*, 1946) and played the son of Takashi Shimura's cancer-stricken father in Akira Kurosawa's *Ikiru* (1952).

In 1954 Kaneko joined Nikkatsu as a contract player, though he continued to work for other studios. From 1956, however, he appeared in Nikkatsu films almost exclusively, making as many as twenty a year in a variety of roles.

Once production of Nikkatsu Action films moved into full swing in 1958 and 1959, Kaneko became the genre's all-purpose bad guy, playing the leader of a Kobe smuggling ring in *Guitar Wanderer* (*Guitar o Motta Wataridori*, 1959), the unscrupulous real estate developer in *Plains Wanderer* (*Daisogen no Wataridori*, 1960) and the shifty saloon boss in *Fast-Draw Guy* (*Hayauchi Yaro*, 1961). His villains tended to be intellectual types with an explosive streak, but Kaneko could also give them a comic spin, as he proved playing the crooked-but-credulous shipping company boss in *Dirty Work* (*Rokudenashi Kagyo*, 1961).

In 1963, after the peak of the Nikkatsu Action boom passed, Kaneko again began to work for other studios, including Daiei and Toei, particularly in the latter's gang films. Among his best remembered roles was the craven-but-calculating gang boss Yamamori in Kinji Fukasaku's *Battles Without Honour and Humanity* (*Jingi naki Tatakai*, 1973-74) series.

After the popularity of the yakuza genre faded in the mid-1970s, Kaneko continued to work steadily in films, plays and television. An enthusiastic gourmet and amateur chef, he also appeared on cooking shows and penned essays on his gastronomic adventures. On 20 January, 1995 he died of heart failure, at the age of seventy one.

Nobuo Kaneko Selected Filmography

The Descendants of Urashima Taro (*Urashima Taro no Koei*, 1946)
Ikiru (1952)
Guitar Wanderer (*Guitar o Motta Wataridori*, 1959)
Plains Wanderer (*Daisogen no Wataridori*, 1960)
Fast-Draw Guy (*Hayauchi Yaro*, 1961)
Dirty Work (*Rokudenashi Kagyo*, 1961)
Battles Without Honour and Humanity (*Jingi naki Tatakai*, 1973)

No Borders, No Limits

Nobuo Kaneko.

Tamio Kawachi (1938-)

A versatile, volatile cinematic talent in his youth, whose characters typically ranged from bright-eyed adolescents to wised-up punks, Tamio Kawachi was born in Kanagawa Prefecture in 1938. He joined the Nikkatsu studio in 1957, after he had dropped out of Kanto Gakuin University, and soon made his debut in Tomotaka Tasaka's *A Slope in the Sun* (*Hi no Ataru Sakamichi*, 1958), in which he played the role of Yujiro Ishihara's mercurical half-brother. He made an immediate favourable impression with his uninhibited performance of the film's rocking theme song.

He was promoted, together with Akira Kobayashi and Tadao Sawamoto, as a member of Nikkatsu's *San Aku Trio* (Bad Boy Trio) and was soon appearing regularly in the studio's action and youth films. Among his best – and certainly most unusual – work of this period was his striking performance in Koreyoshi Kurahara's *Season of Heat* (*Kyonetsu no Kisetsu*, 1960). Playing a jazz-obsessed delinquent who acts unhesitatingly on his criminal impulses, Kawachi dominated the screen with his feral energy and jive-bopping grace, like a Neal "On the Road" Cassady who could act. He later reprised this jazzbo character in Kurahara's *Black Sun* (*Kuroi Taiyo*, 1964).

As he grew out of his punk phase, the studio began giving him a wider range of roles, including the sadistic homosexual in Seijun Suzuki's *Youth of the Beast* (*Yaju no Seishun*, 1963). He appeared frequently in Suzuki's films thereafter: as the man of mystery with the mask and cape in *The Flower and the Angry Waves (Hana to Doto*, 1964); the pure-hearted soldier who falls in love with an army prostitute in *Story of a Prostitute* (*Shunpu-den*, 1965); and the slithery hitman who pursues Tetsuya Watari's hero in *Tokyo Drifter* (*Tokyo Nagaremono*, 1966).

He also lent his distinctive, versatile presence to the Nikkatsu New Action films of the late 1960s, including Yasuharu Hasebe's *Retaliation* (*Shima wa Moratta*, 1968) and *Savage Wolf Pack* (*Yaju o Kese*, 1969).

After Nikkatsu New Action's decline, Kawachi made the move to Toei, where he appeared in the seven-part *Viper Brothers* (*Mamushi no Kyodai*, 1971-74) series with Bunta Sugawara, adding comedy to his acting repertoire. After that experience, he continued to work steadily as a second lead or supporting actor for the likes of Toru Kawashima in *Chi*n*pi*ra* (1984), Takahito Hara in *Town of Beauties* (*Beppin no Machi*, 1989), Hideo Gosha in *Heat Wave* (*Kagero*, 1991) and other directors, though his film roles became fewer in the 1990s. In 2003, he made an appearance under his own name in Takashi Miike's *Gozu* (*Gokudo Kyofu Daigekijo: Gozu*).

Tamio Kawachi and Noriko Matsumoto feel the long arm of the law in "Season of Heat" (Kyonetsu no Kisetsu, 1960).

Tamio Kawachi Selected Filmography

A Slope in the Sun (*Hi no Ataru Sakamichi*, 1958)
Season of Heat (aka *Warped Ones*) (*Kyonetsu no Kisetsu*, 1960)
Black Sun (*Kuroi Taiyo*, 1964)
Youth of the Beast (*Yaju no Seishun*, 1963)
The Flower and the Angry Waves (*Hana to Doto*, 1964)
Story of a Prostitute (*Shunpu-den*, 1965)
Tokyo Drifter (*Tokyo Nagaremono*, 1966)
Retaliation (*Shima wa Moratta*, 1968)
Savage Wolf Pack (*Yaju o Kese*, 1969)
Guys Behind Bars: Viper Brothers (*Choeki Yaro: Mamushi no Kyodai*, 1971)

Hideki Takahashi (1944-)

A frequent presence in Nikkatsu Action films, though his pure-spirited macho persona proved better suited for the *ninkyo* gangster genre, Hideki Takahashi was born in Kisarazu, Chiba Prefecture in 1944. He passed the fifth New Faces audition in May 1961, while still in high school, and made his screen debut that August in Akira Kobayashi's *Children of the Highlands* (*Kogenji*).

This was a year of turmoil for Nikkatsu, with Yujiro Ishihara injured in a skiing accident in January and Keiichiro Akagi killed in a go-cart crash in February. The studio needed new talent to fill two big gaps – and the tall, handsome, athletic Takahashi was enlisted, getting a major role with his second film, *Kidnapping in Broad Daylight* (*Mahiru no Yukai*, 1961). His work with Ruriko Asaoka in the romantic drama *The Dojokko Song* (*Dojokko no Uta*, 1961) boosted his popularity and in 1962 he was elevated to the Green Line of youth film stars, together with Sayuri Yoshinaga and Mitsuo Hamada.

After playing the elder brother of Hamada in Toshio Masuda's *Walk with Your Chin Up* (*Ue o Mite Aruko*, 1962), Takahashi filled in for the deceased Akagi as a boxer-turned-sailor in *The Man Who Lives in the Torrent* (*Gekiryu ni Ikiru Otoko*, 1962). The success of this film made him a stand-alone star and Nikkatsu began using him in more action vehicles, while continuing to cast him in youth films to appeal to his female fans, including remakes of the classics *Blue Mountains* (*Aoi Sanmyaku*, 1963) and *Izu Dancer* (*Izu no Odoriko*, 1963).

Takahashi, however, never quite broke into the Nikkatsu Action elite. Instead the film that boosted him to the top was Akinori Matsuo's *Symbol of a Man* (*Otoko no Monsho*, 1963), in which he played an earnest young doctor who takes over his father's gang after the old man's murder by a rival. A smash hit, it helped ignite the *ninkyo* film boom and generated a ten-part series, with Takahashi playing the lead in all instalments. He became Nikkatsu biggest *ninkyo* star, while dropping out of the youth film line-up.

Takahashi also starred in Seijun Suzuki's *Our Blood Will Not Allow It* (*Oretachi no Chi ga Yurusanai*, 1964) as the free-spirited younger brother to Akira Kobayashi's world-weary gangster, in *Tattooed Life (Irezumi Ichidai*, 1965) as a gangster on the run with his artist brother, and in *Elegy to Violence (Kenka Elegy*, 1966) as a sexually frustrated, full-of-beans student who spends his days fighting and, in one memorable scene, plays his inamorata's piano with his erection.

In 1968 Takahashi made his first appearance on television in the hit NHK maxi-drama *Ryoma Comes* (*Ryoma ga Yuku*), launching a new career as a TV period drama star. In 1969 he left Nikkatsu to become a freelancer and found starring roles in the Tai Kato period dramas *Theatre of Life* (*Jinsei Gekijo*, 1972) and *Miyamoto Musashi* (1973). After 1975, he left the film world for good, his only screen appearance since being in Kosaku Yamashita's 1988 spy drama *Another Way: D Group Information* (*Another Way D Kikan Joho*). Meanwhile, he became a familiar face on television dramas and variety shows.

Starting in 1968, Takahashi acted occasionally in plays, principally period dramas, and in 1978 started his own production company, A-I-U-E-O, for the vowel sounds in Japanese. A fervent golf and shoji (Japanese chess) player, teetotaler and workaholic, Takahashi is said to be the same straight-arrow off the screen as he was on.

Hideki Takahashi Selected Filmography

Children of the Highlands (*Kogenji*, 1961)
Kidnapping in Broad Daylight (*Mahiru no Yukai*, 1961)
The Dojokko Song (*Dojokko no Uta*, 1961)
Walk with Your Chin Up (*Ue o Mite Aruko*, 1962)
The Man Who Lives in the Torrent (*Gekiryu ni Ikiru Otoko*, 1962)
Blue Mountains (*Aoi Sanmyaku*, 1963)
Izu Dancer (*Izu no Odoriko*, 1963)
Symbol of a Man (*Otoko no Monsho*, 1963)
Our Blood Will Not Allow It (*Oretachi no Chi ga Yurusanai*, 1964)
Tattooed Life (*Irezumi Ichidai*, 1965)
Elegy to Violence (*Kenka Elegy*, 1966)
Ryoma Comes (*Ryoma ga Yuku*) (TV series)
Theatre of Life (*Jinsei Gekijo*, 1972)
Miyamoto Musashi (1973)
Another Way: D Group Information (*Another Way D Kikan Joho*, 1988)

right: Hideki Takahashi.

Original theatrical poster for "Our Blood Will Not Allow It" (Oretachi no Chi Ga Yurusanai, 1964), starring Hideki Takahashi *(left)* and Akira Kobayashi *(right)*.

　　　　　　　　　　　　No Borders, No Limits

Original theatrical poster for "Velvet Hustler" (Kurenai no Nagareboshi, 1967), starring Tatsuya Fuji.

Tatsuya Fuji (1941-)

A Nikkatsu New Action star, whose thrill-seeking, authority-defying punks and bikers defined the genre, Tatsuya Fuji was born in Beijing, China in 1941. While still a student in the theatre course of Nihon University's Arts Department, he was scouted by Nikkatsu and joined the studio in 1962. In October of that year he made his debut in *Hometown Sea (Bokyo no Umi)*. Over the next several years, Fuji appeared in a steady stream of films, including Koreyoshi Kurahara's experimental East-meets-West drama *Black Sun (Kuroi Taiyo*, 1964) and Mitsuo Ezaki's mood action classic *Black Strait (Kuroi Kaikyo*, 1964), but made little impression.

In his 38th film, the 1966 remake of the 1957 Yujiro Ishihara hit *The Guy Who Started a Storm (Arashi o Yobu Otoko)*, Fuji finally got his break playing the younger brother of Tetsuya Watari's hard-living jazz drummer. He continued his rise, portraying the nervy gangster brother of Joe Shishido's disco manager in *Slaughter Gun (Minagoroshi no Kenju*, 1967), the indefatigable detective pursuing Watari in *Velvet Hustler (Kurenai no Nagareboshi*, 1967) and the bumbling gangster sidekick to Akira Kobayashi's opportunistic hood in *Roughneck (Arakure*, 1969). In *Bloody Territories (Koiki Boryoku: Ryuketsu no Shima*, 1969), Fuji played a gangster who seems to be an indolent, cat-stroking decadent, until he explodes into deadly violence against his enemies.

In the brief heyday of Nikkatsu New Action in the early 1970s, Fuji finally emerged as a star in his own right. He played a biker gang leader in the five-part *Stray Cat Rock (Nora Neko Rock)* series and one of the *chinpira* who, betrayed by their own gang, seek revenge in Yukihiro Sawada's *Attack (Nagurikomi*, 1970). In these and other New Action roles Fuji expressed the spirit of the times, in which hippie idealism had died, but hippie hedonism and rebellion were still alive and well, especially in the criminal classes. His bikers and gangsters were no Easy Riders seeking new spiritual frontiers (or Shangri Las for getting high and dropping out). Instead, they were sociopaths who got by on nerve and attitude in a world with no rules, save the eternal one of eat or be eaten.

In 1972, following Nikkatsu's collapse, Fuji left the studio and became a freelancer. He made frequent appearances in Toei yakuza films, including three instalments of the 16-part *Wolves of the City (Furyo Bancho*, 1968-1972) comic action series about a scruffy biker gang. In Nagisa Oshima's *In the Realm of the Senses (Ai no Corrida*, 1976) he played the innkeeper lover of a sex-mad maid who lovingly strangles and tenderly castrates him in the notorious climax. The film became an international cause célèbre, as censors in Japan and elsewhere wrestled with (or simply smeared gel over) its full frontal nudity, while critics proclaimed it a transgressive masterpiece. Fuji also starred in Oshima's less successful follow-up, *Empire of Passion (Ai no Borei*, 1978).

In the 1980s, propelled by his *In the Realm of the Senses* notoriety, Fuji appeared in films by leading indie directors, including Shinji Somai's *PP Rider* (*Shonben Rider*, 1983), Yoichi Sai's *Sleep Well, My Friend* (*Tomo yo Shizuka ni Nemure*, 1985) and Azuma Morisaki's *Guys Who Never Learn* (*Hei no Naka no Korenai Menmen*, 1987). Recent films include Takashi Miike's *The Man in White* (*Yurusarezaru Mono*, 2003), Kiyoshi Kurosawa's *Bright Future* (*Akarui Mirai*, 2003) and Song Hae-sung's *Rikidozan* (*Yeokdosan*, 2005).

Tatsuya Fuji Selected Filmography

Hometown Sea (*Bokyo no Umi*, 1962)
Black Sun (*Kuroi Taiyo*, 1964)
The Guy Who Started a Storm (*Arashi o Yobu Otoko*, 1966)
Slaughter Gun (*Minagoroshi no Kenju*, 1967)
Velvet Hustler (*Kurenai no Nagareboshi*, 1967)
Roughneck (*Arakure*, 1969)
Bloody Territories (*Koiki Boryoku: Ryuketsu no Shima*, 1969)
Stray Cat Rock: Sex Hunter (*Nora Neko Rock: Sex Hunter*, 1970)
Attack (*Nagurikomi*, 1970)
Wolves of the City: The Round Up (*Furyo Bancho: Ichimo Daijin*, 1972)
In the Realm of the Senses (*Ai no Corrida*, 1976)
Empire of Passion (*Ai no Borei*, 1978)
PP Rider (*Shonben Rider*, 1983)
Sleep Well, My Friend (*Tomo yo Shizuka ni Nemure*, 1985)
Guys Who Never Learn (*Hei no Naka no Korenai Menmen*, 1987)
The Man in White (*Yurusarezaru Mono*, 2003)
Bright Future (*Akarui Mirai*, 2003)
Rikidozan (*Yeokdosan*, 2005)

top: Tatsuya Fuji *(left)*, Jiro Okazaki *(centre)* and Joe Shishido *(right)* are brothers in arms in "Slaughter Gun" (Minagoroshi no Kenju, 1967).

THE DIRECTORS:
MASUDA, KURAHARA, SUZUKI and HASEBE

Toshio Masuda (1927-)

Nikkatsu's top director of action films, who worked with the studio's biggest stars, while shaping genre styles, Toshio Masuda was born in Kobe in 1927, the son of a seaman. A free-spirited youth, Masuda resisted military indoctrination at a technical training school and was expelled in July 1945. He soon entered the Russian Department of the Osaka University of Foreign Studies to specialise in Russian literature. There he became a fan of French films, while attempting to master the intricacies of Russian grammar (a struggle he ultimately abandoned).

In 1949, after graduation, Masuda went to Tokyo where he studied at the Scenario Academy of the Shin Toho Studio. In August 1950 he joined Shin Toho and worked as an assistant director under Umetsugu Inoue, Nobuo Nakagawa and Mikio Naruse, while continuing to write screenplays.

At the end of 1954 he followed Inoue to Nikkatsu, where he wrote scripts for his mentor's films, including *Lunar Eclipse* (*Gesshoku*, 1957) and *The Winner* (*Shorisha*, 1957) and co-wrote *The Eagle and the Hawk* (*Washi to Taka*, 1957). He also worked as an assistant director on Kon Ichikawa's *The Heart* (*Kokoro*, 1955) and *The Harp of Burma* (*Burma no Tategoto*, 1956). In October 1957 he was promoted to director and debuted in 1958 with *A Journey of Body and Soul* (*Kokoro to Niku no Tabi*).

Masuda had his first major hit with his third film, *Rusty Knife* (*Sabita Knife*, 1958). Based on a script by Shintaro Ishihara, the film starred Yujiro Ishihara and Akira Kobayashi as two *chinpira* who witness a murder – and are pursued by the killers even after they try to go straight. The film thrilled audiences with its fast-paced mix of mystery and action, as well its dramatic climactic chase involving two duelling dump trucks.

Masuda followed with *Red Quay* (*Akai Hatoba*, 1958) a moody thriller based on *Pépé le Moko*, again starring Ishihara, and *The Perfect Game* (*Kanzen na Yugi*, 1958), an intricately plotted thriller about college students who commit the perfect crime, with unintended consequences. Kobayashi plays the hero, torn between his conscience and the cheerful amorality of his conniving friends.

In 1959 Masuda made *Live for Today* (*Kyo ni Ikiru*), a reworking of *Shane*, with Ishihara as a drifter who cleans up a rough mining town. The film laid the groundwork for the studio's trademark *Wanderer* (*Wataridori*) series.

Original theatrical poster for Toshio Masuda's "Red Handkerchief" (Akai Handkerchief, 1964).

He worked with Yujiro Ishihara again during 1959, on *The Man Who Risked Heaven and Earth* (*Ten to Chi o Kakeru Otoko*), a thriller about a death-defying pilot. In all, Masuda ended up making twenty five films with Japan's most popular star – the largest number of any Nikkatsu director and an indication of his high status in the studio pecking order. (Colleague Seijun Suzuki , on the other hand, never made one.)

Among the biggest hits of this collaboration was *Red Handkerchief* (*Akai Handkerchief*, 1964), which starred Ishihara as a Yokohama detective who shoots and kills the father of the woman he loves, a factory girl played by Ruriko Asaoka. He quits the force and becomes a construction worker – but the past, as well as a persistent cop played by Nobuo Kaneko, finally brings him back to Yokohama, where he tries to discover the truth of what happened that fateful day.

Several scenes, including a passionate reunion between Ishihara and Asaoka in Ishihara's seedy hotel room, have a ripe romanticism, soaked in noir atmospherics, that makes comparisons with *Casablanca* not absurd. *Red Handkerchief* not only set the pattern for the mood action films to come, but was also the third-highest earning Japanese film of 1964.

Another major Masuda hit was *Hana and Ryu* (*Hana to Ryu*, 1962), in which Ishihara plays a gangster who loses his passage money to Brazil gambling and, while earning it back, becomes involved with two women. Set at the end of the Meiji period (1868-1912), the film was Ishihara's first period drama and became Nikkatsu's number one hit for the year. It also was a precursor of the *ninkyo* film genre that was to become hugely popular the following year – and remain so through most of the decade.

Masuda often worked with Akira Kobayashi, beginning with *Rusty Knife* – the film that made him a star. He also directed Kobayashi in his first leading role, as a college boy who discovers the harshness of the real world in *The Perfect Game*.

In 1967, with *Velvet Hustler* (*Kurenai no Nagareboshi*), Masuda boosted yet another Nikkatsu hope, Tetsuya Watari, to stardom. Watari played a happy-go-lucky hitman, hiding out in Kobe, who trades flirty quips with the sharp-tongued rich girl played by Ruriko Asaoka, who is supposed to be looking for her missing fiancée. A loose remake of *Red Quay*, shot with more brio and humour than the original, the film was a change of pace for both director and star.

More typical of Masuda and Watari's work together was *Gangster VIP* (*Burai Yori Daikanbu*, 1968), the first entry in the actor's signature *Hoodlum* (*Burai*) series. Based on the reminiscences of real-life yakuza Goro Fujita, the film starred Watari as a lone-wolf gangster who lives by his own code and uses a short sword as his weapon of choice. Once again Masuda delivered taut action, as well as a riveting finale, beginning with a desperate fight in a nightclub backroom between Watari and enemy hoods. The on-screen action unfolds without the customary shouts and grunts – the only sound coming from a female singer who is crooning obliviously in the next room. The film served as a template for the Nikkatsu New Action sub-genre.

In 1968, after helming fifty three films for Nikkatsu, Masuda became a freelancer, but continued to work steadily. In 1970, he and Kinji Fukasaku directed the Japanese scenes for the 20th Century Fox war drama *Tora! Tora! Tora!* after Akira Kurosawa deboarded the project.

Over the next two decades, his reputation as a hitmaker firmly established, Masuda was hired for a succession of major studio projects, including *Catastrophe 1999: The Prophecies of Nostradamus* (*Nostradamus no Daiyogen*, 1974) and three big-budget war movies for Toei: *The Battle of Port Arthur* (*Kochi 203*, 1980), *The Great Japanese Empire* (*Dainippon Teikoku*, 1982) and *The Battle of the Sea of Japan: To Go to Sea* (*Nihonkai Daikaisen: Umi Yukeba*, 1983).

He also tried his hand at other genres, making the teen-targeted *High Teen Boogie* (1982), about a biker who falls in love with a straight girl, and *Company Funeral* (*Shaso*, 1989), a drama about a corporate succession struggle that was selected for the *Kinema Junpo* annual Best Ten list. His most unusual project during this period were five animated films in the *Space Battleship Yamato* (*Uchu Senkan Yamato*) series (1977-1983), which he directed in collaboration with series creator Leiji Matsumoto.

Masuda's most recent feature was the 1992 crime thriller *Heavenly Sin* (*Tengoku no Taizai*), starring Omar Sharif as a Chinese mafia boss and Sayuri Yoshinaga as a detective in a near future Tokyo. Though it opened the Tokyo International Film Festival, the film was bashed critically and failed commercially. One problem was the casting: Sharif was a replacement for Yusaku Matsuda, dead at the age of forty from cancer, who might have been more convincing as both the boss and Yoshinaga's love interest. Since then Masuda has been active in television, both as a director and scriptwriter.

In his Nikkatsu period, Masuda was a leader in defining studio style, from borderless action's Eastern Western atmospherics to the mood action mix of danger and romance. He borrowed from European and Hollywood sources, but localised them so the young Japanese audience could identify – and dream.

In the process, he made films that were not only box office hits in their day, but are also still affectionately remembered by Japanese fans and regarded by Japanese critics as genre landmarks. In the industry, Masuda has a reputation as a pro's pro, who not only consistently delivered strong work in the tough conditions of the Nikkatsu movie factory, but also continued to have a flourishing career for decades after the studio system collapsed.

日㋝活　赤いハンカチ

Hideaki Nitani *(left)* and Yujiro Ishihara mix it up in Toshio Masuda's "Red Handkerchief" (Akai Handkerchief, 1964).

Toshio Masuda Filmography

A Journey of Body and Soul (*Kokoro to Niku no Tabi*, 1958)
National Highway Number Two in the Night Fog (*Yogiri no Daini Kokudo*, 1958)
Rusty Knife (*Sabita Knife*, 1958)
Leaving Haneda at 7:50 (*Hanedahatsu 7-ji 50-pun*, 1958)
Red Quay (*Akai Hatoba*, 1958)
The Perfect Game (*Kanzen na Yugi*, 1958)
Forget About Women (*Onna o Wasurero*, 1959)
Live for Today (*Kyo ni Ikiru*, 1959)
The Man Explodes (*Otoko ga Bakuhatsu Suru*, 1959)
The Man Who Risked Heaven and Earth (*Ten to Chi o Kakeru Otoko*, 1959)
Yakuza Song (*Yakuza no Uta*, 1960)
Tree of Youth (*Seinen no Ki*, 1960)
The Brawler (*Kenka Taro*, 1960)
Man at the Bullfight (*Togyu ni Kakeru Otoko*, 1960)
The Stray Dog That Was Alive (*Ikiteita Nora Inu*, 1961)
Bodyguard Work (*Yojimbo Kagyo*, 1961)
When the Sun Colours the Sea (*Taiyo: Umi o Someteiru Toki*, 1961)
The Sun Is Mad (*Taiyo wa Kurutteiru*, 1961)
Quiet Man of the Underworld (*Ankokugai no Shizukana Otoko*, 1961)
The Town Where Man Lived with Man (*Otoko to Otoko no Ikiru Machi*, 1962)
Walk with Your Chin Up (*Ue o Muite Aruko*, 1962)
The House of Black Cloud Zero Fighters (*Reisen Kurokumo Ikka*, 1962)
Two Lonely People (*Hitoribochi no Futari Da ga*, 1962)
Hana and Ryu (*Hana to Ryu*, 1962)
Escape to the Sun (*Taiyo e Dasshutsu*, 1963)
Prince of Wolves (*Okami no Oji*, 1963)
Red Handkerchief (*Akai Handkerchief*, 1964)
Theatre of Life (*Jinsei Gekijo*, 1964)
Lowly Bugs by the River (*Kawauchi-zoro Dokechi Mushi*, 1964)
Kill the Killer (*Satsujinsha o Kese*, 1964)
Fighting Birds by the River (*Kawauchi-zoro Kenka Gunkei*, 1964)
White Bird (*Shirotori*, 1965)
What Is Youth! (*Seishun wa Nanda*, 1965)
Duel in the Red Valley (*Akai Tanima no Ketto*, 1966)
Tales of Japanese Chivalry: Invitation to a Bloodbath (*Nihon Ninkyoden Chimatsuri Kenkajo*, 1966)
Kill the Night Rose (*Yoru no Bara o Kese*, 1966)
Challenge to Glory (*Eiko e no Chosen*, 1966)
The Guy Who Started a Storm (*Arashi o Yobu Otoko*, 1966)
Stars, Don't Cry: The Winning Guy (*Hoshi yo Nakuna Shori no Otoko*, 1967)

The Storm Comes and Goes (*Arashi Kitari Saru*, 1967)
Friendly Enemies (*Taiketsu*, 1967)
Velvet Hustler (*Kurenai no Nagareboshi*, 1967)
The Endless Duel (*Ketto*, 1967)
Gangster VIP (*Burai Yori Daikanbu*, 1968)
Story of My Life: Enka (*Waga Inochi no Uta: Enka*, 1968)
Stormy Era (*Showa no Inochi*, 1968)
Ah, Tower of Lillies (*Ah Himeyuri no To*, 1968)
Exiled to Hell (*Jigoku no Hamonjo*, 1969)
The Big Boss: Attack! (*Daikanbu Nagurikomi!*, 1969)
The Cleanup (*Arashi no Yushatachi*, 1969)
Tora! Tora! Tora! (1970)
Spartan Education: Go to Hell, Dad (*Sparta Kyoiku Kutabare Oyaji*, 1970)
Battle At Dawn (*Akatsuki no Chosen*, 1971)
Goodbye Gangster Code (*Saraba Okite*, 1971)
Shadow Hunter (*Kage Gari*, 1972)
The Human Revolution (*Ningen Kakumei*, 1973)
Catastrophe 1999: The Prophecies of Nostradamus (*Nostradamus no Daiyogen*, 1974)
The Human Revolution 2 (*Zoku Ningen Kakumei*, 1976)
Space Battleship Yamato (*Uchu Senkan Yamato*, 1977)
Farewell to Space Battleship Yamato: In the Name of Love (*Saraba Uchu Senkan Yamato: Ai no Senshitachi*, 1978)
Take Off (1978)
The Battle of Port Arthur (*Kochi 203*, 1980)
Be Forever, Yamato (*Yamato yo Towa ni*, 1980)
Space Battleship Yamato: The New Voyage (*Uchu Senkan Yamato: Aratanaru Tabidachi*, 1981)
High Teen Boogie (1982)
The Great Japanese Empire (*Dainippon Teikoku*, 1982)
Future War 198X (1982)
Final Yamato (*Uchu Senkan Yamato: Kanketsuhen*, 1983)
The Battle of the Sea of Japan: To Go to Sea (*Nihonkai Daikaisen: Umi Yukeba*, 1983).
L*O*V*Ai NG (*Eru*O*Bui*Ai NG*, 1983)
Zero Fighter in Flames (*Zerosen Moyu*, 1984)
Love: Take Off (*Ai: Tabidachi*, 1985)
Odin (*Odin Koshi Hobune Starlight*, 1985)
The Angel with One Wing (*Katayoku Dake no Tenshi*, 1986)
Tokyo Blackout (*Shuto Shoshitsu*, 1987)
This Story of Love (*Kono Ai no Monogatari*, 1987)
Company Funeral (*Shaso*, 1989)
Sure Death 5: Blood of Gold (*Hissatsu 5: Ogon no Chi*, 1991)
The Great Shogunate Battle (*Edo-jo Tairan*, 1991)
Heavenly Sin (*Tengoku no Taizai*, 1992)

An interview with Toshio Masuda
by Mark Schilling

Q: How did you get into the film industry?

Masuda: Straight from college. This was when everyone was poor and hungry, with little to hope for in a burnt-out world. I devoured French films released during the war – they were shown here on new prints, on beautiful film stock. They had a big impact on me. I knew I would be bored as an ordinary company employee, so I thought I would become a film director instead.

But if my friends hadn't all joined film companies, I never would have become a director. First I studied scriptwriting, then I became an assistant director. Teruo Ishii was the same – we both joined Shin Toho. I was there for about four years, then I went to Nikkatsu. I was an assistant director at Nikkatsu for three years, then I became a director.

above: Toshio Masuda in 2005.

Q: You worked with a lot of different directors when you were an AD.

Masuda: That's right. The one who had the biggest impact on me was Mikio Naruse. At Nikkatsu I worked with Kon Ichikawa. He made *The Harp of Burma* (*Burma no Tategoto*) twice, but I was his first assistant director on the first one. We went to Bangkok on location.

Q: What did you make with Naruse?

Masuda: Naruse made all these great films before the war, but after the war he went into a bit of a slump. When he was at Shin Toho during that period he made two films – *Ginza Cosmetics* (*Ginza Kesho*, 1951) and *Mother* (*Okasan*, 1952). His first assistant director on those films was Teruo Ishii. I was his second.

Q: Ishii told me he learned quite a lot from Naruse – that he could always rely on Naruse's technique when he was stuck.

Masuda: That's probably right, but their styles of filmmaking are totally different.

Q: Did Ichikawa also have a big impact on you?

Masuda: Not really – we're different types, but I did learn how to use the camera from him. Then I worked with Umetsugu Inoue, who made *The Guy Who Started a Storm* (*Arashi o Yobu Otoko*, 1957). He was like an older brother to me.

Q: He made all those Sun Tribe movies.

Masuda: That's right. *The Guy Who Started a Storm* was the film that made Yujiro Ishihara a star. Before that Inoue made *The Eagle and the Hawk* (*Washi to Taka*, 1957) and *The Winner* (*Shorisha*, 1957) – *The Guy Who Started a Storm* was his big break.

Q: How were you influenced by him?

Masuda: He was also a very different type from me. I first met him when he bought a new house. We started writing scripts together and I moved in with him. I wrote rough drafts for several of his scripts. He made films less as dramas than as shows. He would work up these big set-pieces, then link them together. I'm not like that – I'm more interested in people. In any case, a director has to show the audience something – he has to get their attention. So while creating these set-pieces like Inoue's, I would add the drama. That method comes from Inoue's influence.

Q: Nikkatsu Action films nearly always have those set pieces, don't they? There's always a night club scene for example. [laughs] Was Inoue the one who developed that studio style?

Masuda: It wasn't like it is today – night clubs were everywhere then, so those films were telling the truth. But Inoue may be the one who came up with that particular style.

*Q: The most well-known of your early films is **Rusty Knife** (**Sabita Knife**).*

Masuda: I used Akira Kobayashi as Yujiro Ishihara's younger brother in that one. That film made Akira a star.

Q: I was a bit surprised to find out how young you were when you made that film – just thirty. That seemed to be a big project, with the studio's biggest star, to be given to a young director.

Masuda: The studio itself was young. Nikkatsu was an old company, but during the war it was forced to merge with other film companies and stop production. After the war it only distributed foreign films. Then in 1954 it started production again. It recruited directors and stars from several other companies and made some good films, but the company wasn't doing well financially.

Then Yujiro Ishihara came along in *Season of the Sun (Taiyo no Kisetsu)*. The studio thought he was an interesting guy and audiences flocked to see him. So the studio decided to go with young actors and have young directors make their films. That included me, Koreyoshi Kurahara and others.

I was promoted to director when I was twenty nine and I turned thirty while I was making my first film. You ask me why they chose such a young director – the reason is that the studio had new young stars, including Yujiro, and they wanted to make new types of films with them.

*Q: **Rusty Knife** struck me as different from other Japanese action films being made then – more European, perhaps. Was that your aim from the beginning, to make something different?*

Masuda: That's right – I didn't feel there was any point in making the same thing as everyone else. This is a bit off the point, but when *The Guy Who Started a Storm* came out in the New Year's season of that year, Yujiro really took off – fans flocked to see him. Then we heard that a great director named Tomotaka Tasaka was going to bring out *A Slope in the Sun* (*Hi no Ataru Sakamichi*, 1958) for Golden Week [Note: a cluster of holidays in late April and early May]. So Yujiro was taken by Tasaka. The theatre owners in the provinces couldn't believe that a guy who drew the fans the way he did wouldn't have anything out from New Year's to Golden Week – they said it was a waste. So the studio ordered me to put together something in ten days.

The producer who brought me the script was a woman – Takiko Mizunoe. She had been a big star at Shochiku. She was the one who scouted Yujiro. She also found Shintaro (Yujiro's older brother), the current governor of Tokyo. He had written a novel called *Season of the Sun* and suddenly became a big star with it. She asked me to read a script that Shintaro had written. When I looked at it I saw that it was really long – it would take from March to the fall or winter to shoot, but I only had ten days to make it. So I had to redo it and even then I couldn't shoot it in ten days. It took me twelve or thirteen days to make it with Yujiro.

Q: Did you feel a lot of pressure, not just because of the schedule, but also because you were working with a big star?

Masuda: Not really – the only thing I could do was make it the way I liked. I got along well with Yujiro and his older brother Shintaro. I knew Yujiro from when I was an assistant director – I worked on *The Winner* and *The Eagle and the Hawk* with Umetsugu Inoue. We got along really well so I didn't feel any pressure. Both of us were big drinkers. [laughs] Yujiro could really hold his liquor. [laughs]

Q: Did he ask you to write his character a certain way?

Masuda: He never asked me that sort of thing – that wasn't his style. He changed when he got older, but when he was young, he never said that sort of thing.

Q: He became an actor straight out of college, so he didn't have any training, did he?

Masuda: He was a natural. So when I was making a film with Yujiro I made it to suit him. A big star is what he is. He doesn't have to do anything to be a big star – he just is one.

Q: Marlon Brando and James Dean were role models for actors in Hollywood then. Did they have any impact on Yujiro?

Masuda: Not really. Both James Dean and Marlon Brando wanted to be actors and did a lot of work on the stage. Yujiro didn't especially like films or plays. He didn't especially want to become an actor. Tetsuya Watari was the same way.

Q: Even so, he was talkative on the screen compared with Brando and Dean. [laughs] He had a lot of lines in his films.

Masuda: That's the kind of movies they were. He wouldn't memorise his lines the day before shooting – he'd memorise them on the set, in the studio. He had a good memory when he was young.

*Q: **Rusty Knife** and **Red Quay** were something like Hollywood noir. They were shot in Japan, but the settings weren't typically Japanese.*

Masuda: I guess you could say that, but they were still set in Japanese society. Akira Kobayashi's *Guitar Wanderer* (*Guitar o Motta Wataridori*, 1959) was a totally borderless film, but for Yujiro's we adapted the roles to him – this young Japanese guy called Yujiro.

above: Akira Kobayashi *(right)* gets a lesson in the dangers of gang life in "Rusty Knife" (Sabita Knife, 1958).
opposite: Tetsuya Watari cradles a downed hood in "Gangster VIP" (Burai Yori Daikanbu, 1968).

Q: The style was quite different from what Toei was making then – yakuza movies.

Masuda: Toei's were totally different. They had a producer named Koji Shundo who made them that way – dramas about Japanese yakuza. He wouldn't let his people get away from that. We made our films without the studio bosses knowing anything. We dreamed them up to suit ourselves. In other words, we tried to imagine what sort of setting would be good for young people in an action film. Nikkatsu didn't make real yakuza movies. I think of them as "youth films" (*seishun eiga*).

Q: But after Nikkatsu had a big success with the Sun Tribe films, they had problems with them – people criticised the effect the films had on young people.

Masuda: That all started because Yujiro was actually leading the Sun Tribe life. His older brother heard about it from him and turned his story into a novel. But when Yujiro got older he couldn't make Sun Tribe films any more. It became more difficult socially as well. The studio couldn't succeed forever with the Sun Tribe films. For one

thing, the actors couldn't do them forever. They were for the young – by that I mean they expressed a youthful vitality, a youthful rebellion. Yujiro was a kind of punk – that made the Sun Tribe dramas interesting. But as he grew out of that punk phase, it became harder to make dramas based on it.

Q: The Sun Tribe films reflected a contemporary social phenomenon, but when Yujiro moved onto action films, that aspect seemed to be less important, even though they were set in the present. Was it enough for you just to make the films interesting?

Masuda: No – I didn't feel that way. Even action films can say something about the state of the world.

Q: Yujiro played various roles in various types of films, including family dramas – but your films with him were mostly in the action genre. Was that your own preference?

Masuda: More than me liking them, I was asked by the studio to make them. They wanted something that would draw the fans.

Q: Did you have to be especially careful with Yujiro's image? He was such a huge star – I'd think that would have been a concern.

Masuda: When Yujiro was young, he was a guy who stood out. He was a really wonderful person. He was just this young guy, but he was different from all the rest.

Q: He had a long career, but some say he hit his peak before his skiing accident [in 1961].

Masuda: Japanese movies as a whole started to decline then – it wasn't just Yujiro.

Q: That was the time of Nikkatsu's Diamond Line – Yujiro Ishihara, Akira Kobayashi, Keiichiro Akagi, and Koji Wada.

Masuda: Koji Wada was a smaller star than the others, but if Akagi hadn't died that way, he would have gone on a lot longer.

Q: You never worked with him, did you?

Masuda: No – it was really a waste, the way he died.

Q: Ishihara was the heart of the Diamond Line, but after the accident he was out for about seven months. Akagi died – so the studio promoted Joe Shishido...

Masuda: Also, Hideaki Nitani for a while. Then a bit later, Tetsuya Watari. There was also Hideki Takahashi. The studio tried to make those two the successors to Yujiro.

Q: Watari started to come up in 1966 – he appeared with Ishihara in a few films as a kind of younger brother.

Masuda: That's right. After Yujiro started Ishihara Production he kept working for Nikkatsu, but after he went independent he made *Tunnel to the Sun* (*Kurobe no Taiyo*, 1968) and other films outside the studio. The studio needed a second Yujiro, so I made films with Watari that were remakes of Yujiro's hits.

*Q: Before that you made **Red Handkerchief** (**Akai Handkerchief**, 1964). Yujiro and Hideaki Nitani play two detectives who seem at first to be good guys, but you can't really be sure about them, especially Nitani.*

Masuda: He had an intellectual face. He was cast as Yujiro's rival.

Q: You also do something interesting with Ruriko Asaoka, who had an ojosama ("well-bred young lady") image. You had her play a factory girl, with a dirty face. [laughs]

Masuda: You remember that film well. [laughs] A Japanese critic, Takenobu Watanabe – he's a poet who makes a living as an architect – loved Nikkatsu Action and wrote a book about it. He calls *Red Handkerchief* the biggest Nikkatsu Action masterpiece.

Q: Do you agree with that? Is that one your favourites?

Masuda: I don't have favourites. [laughs]

Q: Seijun Suzuki said the same thing when I asked him.

Masuda: Nobody wants to say that kind of thing. [laughs]

Q: You also wrote a lot of the scripts.

Masuda: I didn't especially want to – I had to finish the film so it could be released on a certain month and day. There wasn't time to ask a scriptwriter. After I left Nikkatsu I didn't want to write scripts myself any more. I hired real scriptwriters.

Q: You said Nikkatsu saw Tetsuya Watari as the second Yujiro. What was your impression when you first met him? Did you feel that way too?

Masuda: Yujiro really stood out. I thought that Watari couldn't be as big as Yujiro, but that he could be a good actor.

Q: His image was different from Yujiro's.

Masuda: It was a different era. But both became actors without really wanting to act. Watari was a kid who couldn't act at first. So I told him to be who he was, to act naturally. Yujiro's appeal came from his being something of a punk. He'd been born in a good community, raised in a good family, but there was something of the punk about him. I wonder if that's the right way to put it? Anyway, Watari didn't have that.

Q: He was more the good boy?

Masuda: He was already out of college then, so he wasn't a boy any more. He was really, really serious. He's still a straight-arrow guy.

Q: He was serious about his work?

Masuda: He was serious about life in general. Women were an exception, though. [laughs] He was popular with the ladies. He had the looks of a romantic lead.

Q: Then he appeared in Velvet Hustler (Kurenai no Nagareboshi) as a hitman.

Masuda: He did a good job in that one – he was playing a punk.

*Q: It was a remake of **Red Quay**, but it was quite different.*

Masuda: The hero was a different type. The role itself was different, not just the actor playing it. I wrote the script thinking of Belmondo's character in *Breathless* – that sort of carefree personality. I changed it a bit, though – it wouldn't have been right to make it exactly the same.

*Q: Then Watari made the six-part **Hoodlum** (**Burai**) series.*

Masuda: I only directed the first one, *Gangster VIP* (*Burai Yori Daikanbu*, 1968). That was the best of the lot. A yakuza wrote the book for it. His name was Goro Fujita – he was a real yakuza.

*Q: It reminded me of Kinji Fukasaku's **Battles Without Honour and Humanity** (**Jingi naki Tatakai**, 1973-75) films, which were also based on a real yakuza's memoirs. But your film came a lot earlier.*

Masuda: *Battles Without Honour and Humanity* wasn't the story of one man – it was about these yakuza gangs in Kure. *Gangster VIP* was about one guy named Goro Fujita. It's all Goro's story.

Q: Were you trying to show the reality of the yakuza world?

Masuda: Not really. Basically I was borrowing – I was using the yakuza world as my stage. For me *Gangster VIP* is a youth film. It's about a youth who's gone off the straight and narrow, who's become warped. It's different from Toei's yakuza films. I filmed the hero, not as a yakuza, but as a youth who's become twisted through no fault of his own, who deserves sympathy.

Q: Is that one of your favourite Watari films?

Masuda: I have two – *Velvet Hustler* and *Gangster VIP*. They're totally different, though.

Original theatrical poster for Toshio Masuda's "Duel in the Red Valley" (Akai Tanima no Ketto, 1966).

Tamio Kawachi gets down with Noriko Matsumoto in "Season of Heat" (Kyonetsu no Kisetsu, 1960).　狂熱の季節　1

Koreyoshi Kurahara (1927-2002)

An adventurous, innovative filmmaker in his Nikkatsu years, who later became a mainstream hitmaker with a penchant for directing family movies about animals and foreign locations, Koreyoshi Kurahara was born in 1927 in the province of Sarawak on the island of Borneo, where his father managed a rubber plantation. Following the outbreak of the Pacific War the family left for Tokyo and, as the war situation deteriorated, they were evacuated to a village in Tokushima Prefecture. After graduating from high school, Kurahara joined the navy, but he did not see action.

When the war ended he returned briefly to Tokushima, then entered the Film Department of Nihon University. While still a student he became acquainted with Ishiro Honda, the director of *Godzilla: King of the Monsters* (*Gojira*, 1954). At Honda's introduction, Kurahara became a live-in apprentice of Kajiro Yamamoto, a veteran Toho director who had mentored Akira Kurosawa.

After graduating in 1952, Kurahara became an assistant director at Shochiku's Kyoto Studio. When Nikkatsu resumed production in 1954, he joined the studio and worked under Eisuke Takizawa as an assistant director. In 1957 he made his directorial debut with *I Am Waiting* (*Ore wa Matteiru ze*) starring Yujiro Ishihara. Shot in black-and-white, the film tells the story of a former boxer (Yujiro Ishihara) who saves a young woman (Mie Kitahara) from suicide one foggy night and gives her a job at the restaurant he is managing. He starts to have feelings for her that conflict with his plans to join his brother in Brazil, when he loses her to the gangsters who once owned her. In trying to free her, he learns that they are also the cause of his brother's mysterious silence.

With its port setting, noirish atmosphere and air of being in Japan but not quite of it, *I Am Waiting* became an influential hit, setting the pattern for Nikkatsu Action films to come.

Kurahara followed this success with several other films starring Ishihara. *Ginza Love Story* (*Ginza no Koi no Monogatari*, 1962) paired Ishihara and Ruriko Asaoka in a drama about young lovers who seem to have the world at their feet, until the girl disappears after nearly being killed in a traffic accident. When she finally resurfaces, she has lost her memory – and the most important man in her world has become a stranger.

The film was Nikkatsu's biggest hit of the year and the title song soared to the top of the charts. Kurahara smoothly managed the transition from the light romantic drama of the opening scenes to the darker second half of the film, while stretching his two leads beyond their usual star personas.

Kurahara also directed Ishihara and Asaoka in *That Despicable Guy* (*Nikui Anchikusho*, 1962), which begins as a screwball comedy about the frantic lives of a popular radio DJ (Ishihara) and his manager/lover (Asaoka). Then the DJ decides to abandon his frantic schedule and, as a favour to an attractive stranger (Izumi Ashikawa), personally deliver a jeep to her doctor boyfriend in a remote Kyushu village. An enraged Asaoka pursues him, in his own sports car, the length of Japan.

The comic timing of the opening scenes is spot-on, while the shooting and editing of the long chase sequence has a feeling of wind-in-your-air freedom and headlong propulsion rare in Nikkatsu studio product. Asaoka's occasional lapses into full-blown hysteria are a distraction, but reflect Kurahara's willingness to push his stars out of their comfort zones to new emotional levels – or depths.

During this period Kurahara made several films using not only jazz sound tracks, but also jazzy editing rhythms and camera moves. Unlike Nikkatsu colleague Seijun Suzuki, who used surreal stylistics as a spice for the conventional genre stories of his early 1960s work, Kurahara aimed for consistency of style and content.

Among his boldest departures from studio convention was *Season of Heat* (*Kyonetsu no Kisetsu*, 1960). Tamio Kawachi plays a jazz-crazy delinquent who wreaks twisted revenge on the reporter who sent him to the reformatory, beginning with the rape of his girlfriend. Set to a driving jazz rhythm and shot with a restless, frenetic energy, the film presented its sociopathic hero with none of the conventional moralising.

Kurahara returned to this jazzbo character in *Black Sun* (*Kuroi Taiyo*, 1964), in which he shelters an African-American soldier, who is on the lam after killing a white man in a bar. Once again Kawachi's explosive energy is set to a jazz score, while Kurahara relentlessly strips away his hero's illusions about black Americans in general – and one black American in particular. As the soldier, however, Chico Roland delivers only one note: a piping screech of fear and desperation.

Another departure, in a different direction, was *Glass Johnny: Look Like a Beast* (*Glass no Johnny: Yaju no yo ni Miete*, 1962). Joe Shishido stars as a race track tout whose mission in life is to make a struggling jockey a winner and himself rich. One day he saves a pure-hearted whore (Izumi Ashikawa) who is on the run from her pimp (Ai George). The pimp, however, is persistent – and the tout is less than heroic. When he abandons her, the pimp reclaims her, but ends up wounded and arrested. Instead of making her escape, however, she nurses him. Is she simply a fool and a tool – or something more?

Ashikawa's performance as the whore is reminiscent of Giulietta Masina's in *La strada*, passing beyond victimhood to transcendence, while Kurahara's black-and-white stylisations transform specifics of time, place and culture into a timeless space neither identifiably Japanese nor imitatively Italian.

Original theatrical poster for Koreyoshi Kurahara's "Glass Johnny: Look Like a Beast" (Glass no Johnny: Yaju no yo ni Miete, 1962).

In 1964 Kurahara directed Ruriko Asaoka in *Running Fever* (*Shuen*) – her 100th film since joining Nikkatsu in 1955. Asaoka plays a newlywed whose husband is sent off to war and comes back severely wounded. She nurses him back to health, but he is sent to the front again – and does not return. Asaoka did not give her usual star turn, but a nothing-held-back portrayal of a woman living with loneliness, anxiety and grief – instead of the man she loves. Her performance was hailed as a career peak.

In 1967 Kurahara made *Thirst for Love* (*Ai no Kawaki*), based on the eponymous Yukio Mishima novel. Ruriko Asaoka starred as a widow who continues to live in her father-in-law's house after her husband's death – and falls for a handsome manservant. The film did not please Kurahara's Nikkatsu bosses, who considered it too arty and delayed its release. That same year the director left Nikkatsu and became a freelancer.

Unlike Suzuki, whose career foundered after he was fired by Nikkatsu, Kurahara continued to turn out hits, including *Safari 5000* (*Eiko e no 5,000 Kilo*, 1969) with Yujiro Ishihara and *Rainy Amsterdam* (*Ame no Amsterdam*, 1975) with pop-star-turned-actor Kenichi Hagiwara, both set in foreign locales.

In 1978 he released *The Glacier Fox* (*Kita Kitsune Monogatari*), a documentary about wild foxes in Hokkaido. Its resounding box office success generated a cycle of animal films that would dominate the Japanese market for the next decade. Kurahara contributed to this cycle with *Elephant Story* (*Zo Monogatari*, 1980) and *Antarctica* (*Nankyoku Monogatari*, 1983), the latter based on a true story about dogs left behind by a Japanese expedition to face an Antarctic winter – and the efforts of two expedition scientists to rescue them. Produced by the Fuji TV network, *Antarctica* set a box office record for a Japanese film that was not broken until 1997 by Hayao Miyazaki's *Princess Mononoke* (*Mononoke Hime*). A Hollywood remake, Frank Marshall's *Eight Below*, topped the US box office following its release in February 2006.

After this triumph Kurahara was in great demand, but *To the Sea/See You* (*Umi e/See You*, 1988), a film starring Ken Takakura about the Paris-Dakar Rally, went far over schedule on its African locations and disappointed at the box office. In 1991 he released *Strawberry Road*, a drama based on an autobiographical novel by Yoshimi Ishikawa about his experiences working on a California strawberry farm. Once again Kurahara shot on location, this time for two months in California. Despite a cast that included Toshiro Mifune and Pat Morita, the film did little business on either side of the Pacific.

Although Kurahara did not direct another feature after *Strawberry Road*, he collaborated with Roger Spottiswoode on *Hiroshima* (1995), a three-hour TV drama about the decision to drop the first atomic bomb on Japan, made with documentary footage. Kurahara died of a lung infection on 28 December, 2002.

Koreyoshi Kurahara Selected Filmography

I Am Waiting (*Ore wa Matteiru ze*, 1957)
Season of Heat (aka *Warped Ones*) (*Kyonetsu no Kisetsu*, 1960)
The Jet That Flew Into the Storm (*Arashi o Tsukkiru Jetto-ki*, 1961)
Ginza Love Story (*Ginza no Koi no Monogatari*, 1962)
That Despicable Guy (*Nikui Anchikusho*, 1962)
Glass Johnny: Look Like a Beast (*Glass no Johnny: Yaju no yo ni Miete*, 1962)
Mexican Vagabond (*Mexico Mushuku*, 1962)
Black Sun (*Kuroi Taiyo*, 1964)
Running Fever (*Shuen*, 1964)
A Record of Love and Death (*Ai to Shi no Kiroku*, 1966)
Thirst for Love (*Ai no Kawaki*, 1967)
Safari 5000 (*Eiko e no 5,000 Kilo*, 1969)
Bad Girl Mako (*Furyo Shojo Mako*, 1971)
Sunset, Sunrise (*Hi wa Shizumi, Hi wa Noboru*, 1973)
Rainy Amsterdam (*Ame no Amsterdam*, 1975)
The Glacier Fox (*Kita Kitsune Monogatari*, 1978)
Elephant Story (*Zo Monogatari*, 1980)
Gate of Youth (*Seishun no Mon*, 1981)
Gate of Youth Part 2 (*Seishun no Mon: Jiritsu-hen*, 1982)
Antarctica (*Nankyoku Monogatari*, 1983)
Bell of Spring (*Haru no Kane*, 1985)
To the Sea/See You (*Umi e/See You*, 1988)
Strawberry Road (1991)
Hiroshima (1995)

right: Koreyoshi Kurahara
(Photo from his memorial service, on 19 February, 2003).

Seijun Suzuki (1923-)

The most brilliantly innovative of all Nikkatsu Action directors, Seijun Suzuki was regarded by his studio bosses as a problem child who commercially never quite made the grade. Unlike colleagues Koreyoshi Kurahara and Toshio Masuda, who soared to the top of the studio pecking order while still in their early thirties and gained a measure of organisational clout as a result, Suzuki was a late bloomer, assigned second-tier projects.

He had his successes, including a series of films with teen idol Koji Wada, but didn't truly come into his own until his 28th film as director, *Youth of the Beast* (*Yaju no Seishun*, 1963), a programmer about a cop on a mission that Suzuki transformed into a genre classic with his startling visual inventions and absurdist sense of humour. He continued to experiment, relatively free from studio pressure ("The producers let the director do his job and didn't interfere," he once said. "The set was the director's territory."), but gained only a cult following. He accordingly got little praise from the studio, which wanted crowd-pleasing winners. He finally responded with *Gate of Flesh* (*Nikutai no Mon*, 1964), a bold venture into Eros that drew audiences, but his box office success proved fleeting.

Instead of trying to regain his commercial touch, however, Suzuki made his films ever more Suzuki-esque, until *Branded to Kill* (*Koroshi no Rakuin*, 1967), a convention-shattering exercise in surrealism that played to empty theatres and baffled studio boss Kyusaku Hori, who fired Suzuki – a humiliation for anyone, but especially a veteran director with forty films to his credit. His fans and supporters rose up in protest when Nikkatsu refused to lend Suzuki's films for a career retrospective, but the director was now damaged goods for the other studios. He did not make another feature film for a decade.

Abroad, this narrative of a contrary genius discarded by a soulless studio has come to obscure certain realities of Suzuki's career at Nikkatsu. Firstly, he was no Orson Welles, a prodigy battling the philistines from day one. In the early of years of his directorial career he made movies that were, for the most part, programmers, with little to distinguish them from the run of studio product.

Secondly, when he began, in his late thirties, to make the stylistically unique films that would later establish his reputation abroad, other studio directors had already begun to stretch or redefine genre boundaries, among them Koreyoshi Kurahara with the jazz-inflected, Nouvelle-Vague-ish *Season of Heat* (*Kyonetsu no Kisetsu*, 1960). Another was Takashi Nomura, whose thriller *A Colt Is My Passport* (*Colt wa Ore no Passport*, 1967) was released several months prior to *Branded to Kill* and presaged several elements of Suzuki's far more famous film, including Joe Shishido's

Seijun Suzuki in 2003.

deadpan hitman hero and his stakeout with a sniper rifle. This is not to say that Suzuki was a follower or imitator – his vision was very much his own – but he was also not a lone light in the studio hack darkness.

Born in Tokyo's Sumida Ward on 24 May, 1923, Suzuki was given the first name Seitaro. His father was a manufacturer of bicycle bells, a family business that Suzuki was groomed to inherit. In 1941 he graduated from a Tokyo middle school and took the entrance examination for the Asian Development Institute (*Koa Gakuin*) with the aim of going to Indochina. He failed and studied independently for a year. During this period he saw several films that made a strong impression on him, including Erik Charell's *Congress Dances* (*Der Kongress Tanzt*, 1931) and Hiroshi Inagaki's *The Last Day of Edo Castle* (*Edojo Saigo no Hi*, 1941). He finally entered Hirosaki High School in Aomori Prefecture, but was drafted in December 1943 and started naval officer training.

Assigned to a weather observation unit, he was sent to the Philippines and Taiwan. A transport ship on which he was sailing was sunk by an Allied warplane and he drifted for several days in Philippine waters before being rescued. By the end of the war he had advanced to the rank of Acting Sub-Lieutenant, but had developed a deep distrust of authority, as well as an acute awareness of life's randomness.

Returning to Japan in 1946, Suzuki re-entered Hirosaki High School, from where he graduated in 1948. He took the entrance exam for the University of Tokyo but failed and, at the urging of a friend, entered the film course of the newly founded Kamakura Academy. In September 1948 he passed an assistant director's test at the Shochiku Ofuna studio. He entered Shochiku in October and served as an assistant director on Minoru Shibuya's *Red Lips Not Yet Faded* (*Shushin Imada Kiezu*). He also worked for other directors, but in 1951 was assigned exclusively to Tsuruo Iwama, a melodrama specialist.

In 1954, Suzuki joined Nikkatsu, where he became an AD for several directors, but worked most often with Hiroshi Noguchi, on *My Gun Is Quick* (*Ore no Kenju wa Hayai*, 1954) and other films. Suzuki later called Noguchi his mentor. In 1956 he directed his first film, the musical melodrama *Harbour Toast: Victory Is in Our Grasp* (*Minato no Kanpai: Shori o Wagate ni*, 1956). Beginning with *Underworld Beauty* (*Ankokugai no Bijo*, 1958) he used the professional name Seijun.

In 1959 he directed *The Naked Age* (*Suppadaka no Nenrei*), the film that gave Keiichiro Akagi his first starring role. Suzuki later called film "relatively real." He also made seven films with Koji Wada, the junior member of the Diamond Line of elite male action stars, starting with *Fighting Delinquents* (*Kutabare Gurentai*) in 1960. This second instalment in the comic action *Hoodlums* (*Gurentai*) series was Suzuki's first colour film.

In 1963 Suzuki made the comic actioner *Detective Bureau 2-3: Go to Hell, Bastards* (*Tantei Jimusho 2-3 Kutabare Akuto-domo*) and found a new star in Joe Shishido, whose eccentric tough guy persona was a perfect match for Suzuki's own strange flights of whimsy. The film, about a madcap detective (Shishido) who busts up two yakuza gangs to help a police inspector pal, was a hard-boiled romp that launched Suzuki's cult reputation. In one memorable scene Shishido sings and dances as he sprays machine gun bullets at his enemies.

Suzuki's true breakthrough, however, came with his follow-up, *Youth of the Beast* (1963). Shishido again starred, this time as a disgraced former police detective who poses as a hitman to infiltrate two yakuza gangs and learn the truth about a senior detective's death. Despite the routine story, the flamboyant visuals (e.g. the one-way mirror in a gang-run club that covers the better part of a wall) and outrageous comic action (e.g. the scene of Shishido fighting off baddies while hanging upside down from a chandelier) made it a stand-out.

With his next film, *The Bastard* (*Akutaro*, 1963), Suzuki began an association with art director Takeo Kimura that would enable him to further refine his distinctive style. That year he also shot *Kanto Wanderer* (*Kanto Mushuku*, 1963), his first *ninkyo* film. Akira Kobayashi plays a gambler who becomes involved in the tangled affairs of a reckless young *chinpira* and his savvy older sister – a professional card sharp whose partner is her lantern-jawed husband. Working with Kimura and cameraman Shigeyoshi Mine, Suzuki incorporated Kabuki-esque touches throughout the film. His stylistics reached a height of audacious beauty in the climactic showdown, as primary colours flooded across the screen to express the hero's turbulent emotions.

He incorporated similar elements in *The Flower and the Angry Waves* (*Hana to Doto*, 1964) and *Tattooed Life* (*Irezumi Ichidai*, 1965); films that told conventional tales of gangster outrage and vengeance, while saving the visual pyrotechnics for last.

In the mid-1960s Nikkatsu action films, such as former Suzuki AD Yasuharu Hasebe's *Black Tight Killers* (*Ore ni Sawaru to Abunai ze*, 1966) and Toshio Masuda's *Velvet Hustler* (*Kurenai no Nagareboshi*, 1967) began to reflect shifts in the popular culture toward experimentation and excess, in everything from fashion and music to sex. Suzuki, however, went farther than the rest in *Tokyo Drifter* (*Tokyo Nagaremono*, 1966), making abundant use of Pop Art stylistics, jump cutting with blithe (and, at times, jarring) abandon and staging a barroom brawl inspired by Hollywood Westerns. He didn't subvert the genre so much as explode it.

Tetsuya Watari plays Tetsu Hondo, a gangster whose boss has ostensibly gone straight, but whose former rivals are out to get him. When they grab the deed to the boss's office building, Tetsu goes to his aid – and finds himself overmatched and on the run. Wearing a powder-blue suit and breaking out with the infectious theme song at every opportunity, Tetsu is the ultimate Suzuki action hero, who points up the absurdity around him by barely deigning to notice it.

In his 40th and last film for Nikkatsu, *Branded to Kill* (1967), Suzuki went completely off the genre map into uncharted territory. The plot has to do with the hero's climb up the hitman hierarchy, a job for a sultry client (Annu Mari) that goes disastrously wrong, a deceitful wife (Mariko Ogawa) who nearly does him in and a hitman rival (Koji Nanbara) who takes up where she left off, but Suzuki's interpretation of it is comically, deliriously dream-like, with narrative logic taking a holiday.

The hero, Goro Hanada (Joe Shishido), becomes romantically obsessed with his client and trapped in a contest of wills with his rival that can lead only to death – a fate he is torn between embracing and escaping. Gobbling white rice to boost his virility, he definitely wants to embrace the client – a half-Japanese, half-Indian femme fatale who has a thing for dead birds and butterflies. (One of the former decorates the rear view mirror of her sports car, the latter, the walls of her apartment.)

Hunted by the rival, Hitman Number One (Nanbara), Goro makes a desperate stand in his ultra-moderne flat, sweating and bug-eyed like a trapped animal. In a bizarre twist, he ends up hand-cuffed to Number One, as part of an absurd test of skills and wills. Finally, he accepts an invitation to a mano-a-mano showdown with his nemesis in a boxing arena.

Viewed as a radical deconstruction of the hard-boiled genre or a Kafka-esque essay on the waking nightmare of modern life, *Branded to Kill* makes excellent sense (though Suzuki did not make such interpretations himself). Viewed as a programme picture for action fans, it makes little sense at all, save perhaps as a gesture of defiance or evidence of professional collapse.

Evidently taking the latter view after seeing *Branded to Kill* and its dismal box office returns, Nikkatsu president Kyusaku Hori proclaimed the film "incomprehensible" and fired Suzuki in April 1968. Soon thereafter Nikkatsu denied an organisation called Cineclub Study Group prints for a planned retrospective of his films. This led his supporters, including critics, distributors and others in the film world, to form the Seijun Suzuki Joint Struggle Committee with the aim of demanding Suzuki's reinstatement at Nikkatsu and the use of the prints for the retrospective. Suzuki finally won a court settlement against the studio in 1976, but he found film work hard to come by.

After a decade-long hiatus, he returned to the screen with *A Tale of Sorrow and Sadness* (*Hishu Monogatari*, 1977) for Shochiku, but the film, which depicted the rise and fall of a woman pro golfer, was slated by critics and ignored by fans. By this time, Suzuki was sporting the white goatee that was to become his trademark. He had also shed some of the eccentric personal habits he was known for in his early years as a director, such as never bathing, brushing his teeth or changing his clothes during a shoot.

Suzuki finally made his critical comeback in 1980 with the independently produced *Zigeunerweisen*, a ghost story set in the Taisho period (1912-1926) in which the barriers between the dead and the living dissolve. The film won numerous awards, including the jury prize at the Berlin Film Festival.

Suzuki made two more films in what he called his "Taisho Trilogy": *Heat Shimmer Theatre* (*Kageroza*, 1981) and *Yumeji* (1991). Another film, *Capone Cries a Lot* (*Capone Oi ni Naku*, 1985), is set in nearly the same period, as well as sharing the stylistic quirks of the trilogy's "Suzuki World," but the story – a deluded *naniwabushi* (traditional ballad) singer (Kenichi Hagiwara) goes to America to find fame and fortune – is a trifle and the American sets are a snicker-inducing sham.

In 2001 Suzuki released *Pistol Opera*, a remake of *Branded to Kill* that starred Makiko Esumi as a hitwoman and Mikijiro Hira as an older, wheelchair-bound Goro Hanada. Static and mannered, the film was nonetheless made with Suzuki's characteristic panache and style.

His most recent film is *Princess Raccoon* (*Operetta Tanuki Goten*, 2005), a singing and dancing "operetta" based on a Japanese folk tale, starring Zhang Ziyi as a raccoon dog (*tanuki*) in human form and Joe Odagiri as the prince who falls in love with her. Alternately charming, haunting and tuneful, loaded with CG-generated phantasmagoria, the film is Suzuki's affectionate tribute and farewell to a favourite musical genre and period – the Taisho, when the Japanese operetta was at its peak.

Suzuki has also occasionally acted in other directors' films, playing a version of his puckish, sage-like public personality. He has been ailing of late, however, with respiratory problems aggravated by decades of smoking, and his acting career is in hiatus. He did travel to the Cannes Film Festival in 2005, where *Princess Raccoon* was screened out of competition.

Seijun Suzuki Filmography

Harbour Toast: Victory Is in Our Grasp (*Minato no Kanpai: Shori o Wagate ni*, 1956)
Pure Emotions of the Sea (*Umi no Junjo*, 1956)
Satan's Town (*Akuma no Machi*, 1956)
Inn of the Floating Weeds (*Ukigusa no Yado*, 1957)
Eight Hours of Terror (*Hachijikan no Kyofu*, 1957)
The Naked Woman and the Gun (*Rajo to Kenju*, 1957)
Underworld Beauty (*Ankokugai no Bijo*, 1958)
The Spring That Didn't Come (*Fumihazushita Haru*, 1958)
Young Breasts (*Aoi Chibusa*, 1958)
Voice Without a Shadow (*Kagenaki Koe*, 1958)
Love Letter (1959)
Passport to Darkness (*Ankoku no Ryoken*, 1959)

The Naked Age (*Suppadaka no Nenrei*, 1959)
Aim at the Police Van (*Sono Gososha o Nerae*, 1960)
Sleep of the Beast (*Kemono no Nemuri*, 1960)
Clandestine Zero Line (*Mikko Zero Line*, 1960)
Everything Goes Wrong (*Subete ga Kurutteru*, 1960)
Fighting Delinquents (*Kutabare Gurentai*, 1960)
Tokyo Knights (*Tokyo Kishitai*, 1961)
A Hell of a Guy (*Muteppo Daisho*, 1961)
The Man with the Hollow-Tip Bullets (*Sandanju no Otoko*, 1961)
The Wind-of-Youth Group Crosses the Mountain Pass (*Toge o Wataru Wakai Kaze*, 1961)
Blood-Red Water in the Channel (*Kaikyo, Chi ni Somete*, 1961)
Million Dollar Smash-and-Grab (*Hyakuman Dollar o Tatakidase*, 1961)
High Teen Yakuza (1962)
The Guys Who Put Money on Me (*Ore ni Kaketa Yatsura*, 1962)
Detective Bureau 2-3: Go to Hell, Bastards (*Tantei Jimusho 2-3 Kutabare Akuto-domo*, 1963)
Youth of the Beast (*Yaju no Seishun*, 1963)
The Bastard (*Akutaro*, 1963)
Kanto Wanderer (*Kanto Mushuku*, 1963)
The Flower and the Angry Waves (*Hana to Doto*, 1964)
Gate of Flesh (*Nikutai no Mon*, 1964)
Our Blood Will Not Allow It (*Oretachi no Chi ga Yurusanai*, 1964)
Story of a Prostitute (*Shunpu-den*, 1965)
Stories of Bastards: Born Under a Bad Star (*Akutaroden: Waruihoshi no Shita Demo*, 1965)
Tattooed Life (*Irezumi Ichidai*, 1965)
Carmen from Kawachi (*Kawachi Carmen*, 1966)
Tokyo Drifter (*Tokyo Nagaremono*, 1966)
Elegy to Violence (*Kenka Elegy*, 1966)
Branded to Kill (*Koroshi no Rakuin*, 1967)
There's a Bird Inside a Man (*Otoko no Naka ni wa Tori Ga Iru*, 1969) (TV)
A Mummy's Love (*Mira no Koi*, 1970) (TV)
A Tale of Sorrow and Sadness (*Hishu Monogatari*, 1977)
The Fang in the Hole (*Ana no Kiba*, 1979)
Zigeunerweisen (1980)
Heat Shimmer Theatre (*Kageroza*, 1981)
Lupin III: The Golden Legend of Babylon (*Lupin Sansei: Babiron no Ogon Densetsu*, 1985) (TV series)
Capone Cries a Lot (*Capone Oi ni Naku*, 1985)
Yumeji (1991)
Marriage (*Kekkon*, 1993)
Pistol Opera (2001)
Princess Raccoon (*Operetta Tanuki Goten*, 2005)

right: Seijun Suzuki, in post-Nikkatsu years.

Yasuharu Hasebe (1932-)

The leader of a new generation of Nikkatsu directors in the late 1960s, bringing a fresh, edgy sensibility to stale action product, Yasuharu Hasebe was born in Tokyo's Shinjuku Ward on 4 April, 1932. He entered the French Literature Department of Waseda University in 1950 and on graduation in 1955 joined a publishing company, but soon left to pursue his interest in films. He studied scriptwriting with Kenro Matsuura and in 1958 was hired by Nikkatsu as an assistant director. He worked under Seijun Suzuki on *The Man with the Hollow-Tip Bullets* (*Sandanju no Otoko*), Takashi Nomura on *Blood and Sea* (*Chi to Umi*) and Motomu Ida on *Emergency Measures* (*Hijo Tehai*). He also wrote scripts for several films, including Koreyoshi Kurahara's *Wind Speed, 40 Metres* (*Fusoku 40 Meters*, 1958).

In 1965 Hasebe was promoted to director and in 1966 made his debut feature, *Black Tight Killers* (*Ore ni Sawaru to Abunai ze*). Akira Kobayashi plays a photographer back from the Vietnam War who takes a pretty flight attendant (Chieko Matsubara) to dinner at a jazz club. There she is threatened by a foreigner, who is then killed by a gang of women in black tights, and while the photographer is calling the cops, the flight attendant is snatched and crammed into the trunk of a car.

An international gang, it transpires, is after her deceased father's hidden stash of gold, which he smuggled out of Okinawa after World War II. The women in tights – martial artists from Okinawa – are also after the loot – and the photographer ends up on their side. Filmed with tongue-in-cheek humour and wacky inventiveness (the Okinawans wield 45 rpm records as weapons, among other seemingly non-lethal oddities), *Black Tight Killers* was intended as an action genre spoof and has since become a cult hit in the West. Its resemblance to the wilder work of Hasebe's mentor, Seijun Suzuki, is obvious enough, though it was also in synch with trends in Hollywood and the popular culture at large, where camp was quickly becoming king.

Hasebe's follow-up, *The Guy Called the Bomb Man* (*Bakudan Otoko to Iwareru Aitsu*, 1967), was likewise an action comedy, but his third, *Slaughter Gun* (*Minagoroshi no Kenju*, 1967), was a straight-up action film whose heroes were the three tough-guy brothers, played by Joe Shishido, Tatsuya Fuji and Jiro Okazaki.

After Shishido – the eldest and the manager of a night club – is forced to whack a woman by his gang boss, he quits the gang and ends up fighting a life-or-death battle with it, including a former friend and romantic rival played by Hideaki Nitani. Hard-boiled in the extreme, *Slaughter Gun* was a forerunner of Hasebe's later Nikkatsu New Action films.

Hasebe filmed another dark, unromantic take on underworld life in *Retaliation* (*Shima wa Moratta*, 1968). A gangster (Akira Kobayashi) just out of prison finds his

above: Akira Kobayashi *(left)* faces off in "Roughneck" (Arakure, 1969).

gang fighting a losing battle against an aggressive new rival. Quickly sizing up the situation, he accepts a proposal from the rival boss to eliminate a troublesome third gang and take its territory. The resulting machinations recall those of Toshiro Mifune's *ronin* hero in Akira Kurosawa's *Yojimbo* – and offer the sort of clear look at the dirty realities of yakuza life then uncommon in the genre.

In the 1969 movie *Roughneck* (*Arakure*) Hasebe again broke with genre conventions, in a story about a hoodlum (Akira Kobayashi) who pursues the main chance at every opportunity, even scamming train station officials to avoid paying the fare. Kobayashi shines as the charming scapegrace hero who has no use for the traditional yakuza code of loyalty to the boss and gang. Meanwhile, Hasebe serves up an entertaining mix of black comedy, clever plotting and slashing action.

In 1970 Hasebe directed *Woman Boss: Stray Cat Rock* (*Onna Bancho: Nora Neko Rock*), the first of five instalments in the *Stray Cat Rock* series (1970 to 1971). All five films featured Meiko Kaji as a take-no-crap punk girl and Tatsuya Fuji as the cruel-but-cool leader of a delinquent gang, but did not have a continuing story. Hasebe brought his distinctive flash and dynamism to his three entries, set to a rock beat.

Original theatrical poster for Yasuharu Hasebe's "Black Tight Killers" (Ore ni Sawaru to Abunai ze, 1966).

above: Meiko Kaji *(wearing the hat)* and the gang in "Stray Cat Rock: Sex Hunter" (Nora Neko Rock: Sex Hunter, 1970).

One stand-out is *Stray Cat Rock: Sex Hunter* (*Nora Neko Rock: Sex Hunter*, 1970). Kaji plays the leader of a girl gang that feuds and flirts with the Eagles, thrill-crazy bikers who hang out at a go-go club near the US military base in Tachikawa, Tokyo. The leaders of the two gangs, Mako (Kaji) and Baron (Fuji), are an item – until Baron starts bullying mixed race youths who are part of the scene.

Though the title makes it sound like campy exploitation, *Sex Hunter* explored conflicted Japanese attitudes toward the Americans in their midst – and their *hafu* ("half Japanese") offspring – with more than usual honesty and nuance. Baron, it turns out, is reacting to a black American soldier's rape of his sister. Instead of striking back at the obvious target, however, he becomes the sworn enemy of anyone, male or female, with "impure" blood. Mako becomes the protector of Baron's victims – a mini-skirted fury whom even Baron finds dangerous to cross. He decides to retaliate by inviting Mako's gang to a party and offering the girls as sexual favours to the foreign guests. Chaos ensues, but a rough sort of justice eventually prevails.

In August 1971 Nikkatsu stopped film production, then restarted in November with a new line that came to be called Nikkatsu Roman Porno – erotic fantasies with real characters and plots, usually involving S&M play, but no real penetration.

Hasebe tried his hand at this genre with *Rape!* (*Okasu!*, 1976) and *Assault! Jack the Ripper* (*Boko! Kirisaki Jack*) – films that added a heavy dose of action to the rough sex. He also made *Female Prisoner Sasori: #701's Grudge Song* (*Joshu Sasori 701-go Urami Bushi*) – the fourth instalment in Toei's *Sasori* series, with Kaji playing the title character, an escaped convict who gets unexpected aid from a former student activist with a grudge against the detective who is pursuing her.

In 1980 Hasebe became a freelancer and continued to direct the occasional straight feature film, including the 1982 Kadokawa actioner *Fossil Plain* (*Kaseki no Koya*) and the 1987 Toei cop buddy movie *The Dangerous Detectives* (*Abunai Deka*). His most-recent feature is *Lesson* (*Ressun LESSON*, 1994), a romantic drama starring Tetsuro Watabe as a young journalist and Kumiko Akiyoshi as the older widow he falls in love with.

Since 1969 Hasebe has also directed many films for television broadcast and, since 1990, for video release. He has also written scripts under his pen name, Takashi Fuji.

Yasuharu Hasebe Selected Filmography

Black Tight Killers (*Ore ni Sawaru to Abunai ze*, 1966)
The Guy Called the Bomb Man (*Bakudan Otoko to Iwareru Aitsu*, 1967)
Slaughter Gun (*Minagoroshi no Kenju*, 1967)
Retaliation (*Shima wa Moratta*, 1968)
Roughneck (*Arakure*, 1969)
Bloody Territories (*Koiki Boryoku: Ryuketsu no Shima*, 1969)
Savage Wolf Pack (*Yaju o Kese*, 1969)
Woman Boss: Stray Cat Rock (*Onna Bancho: Nora Neko Rock*, 1970)
Stray Cat Rock: Sex Hunter (*Nora Neko Rock: Sex Hunter*, 1970)
Stray Cat Rock: Machine Animal (*Nora Neko Rock: Machine Animal*, 1970)
Spectreman (1971) TV Series
A Man's World (*Otoko no Sekai*, 1971)
Female Prisoner Scorpion: #701's Grudge Song (*Joshu Sasori: 701-go Urami-bushi*, 1974)
The Horny Detective: Dirty Mari (*Sukeban Deka: Dirty Mari*, 1974)
Sengoku Rock: Female Warriors (*Sengoku Rock Hayate no Onnatachi*, 1974)
Rape! (*Okasu!*, 1976)
Assault! Jack the Ripper (*Boko! Kirisaki Jack*, 1976)
Special Investigations Frontline (*Tokuso Saizensen*, 1977) TV Series
Rape! 25 Hours of Sexual Assault (*Rape! 25-ji Bokan*, 1977)
Secret Honeymoon: Rape Train (*Maruhi Honeymoon: Boko Ressha*, 1977)
Do It! (*Yaru!*, 1978)
Attack! (*Osou!*, 1978)
Erotic Relations (*Erotic na Kankei*, 1978)
Detective Story (*Tantei Monogatari*, 1979) TV Series (episodes 8 and 10)
Fossil Plain (*Kaseki no Koya*, 1982)
The Dangerous Detectives (*Abunai Deka*, 1987)
Lesson (*Ressun LESSON*, 1994)

Original theatrical poster for Yasuharu Hasebe's "Roughneck" (Arakure, 1969).

Original theatrical poster for "Story of Pistol Violence" (Kenju Zankyoku Monogatari, 1964), starring Joe Shishido.
The film's director, Takumi Furukawa, also helmed the first Sun Tribe film, "Season of the Sun" (Taiyo no Kisetsu, 1956).

Glossary

Borderless action (*mukokuseki akushon*):
Nikkatsu action films set in "internationalised" spaces, from Yokohama docks to the wilds of Hokkaido, and featuring protagonists and stories that owe much to Hollywood and European models. The purest examples of borderless action were the Eastern Westerns starring Akira Kobayashi, in which he dressed and acted the part of a Western hero, even though the films were set in contemporary Japan.

Chinpira:
Apprentice gangsters, usually delinquent teenagers, who are at the beck and call of their gang seniors.

Enka:
Soulful minor-key ballads, commonly on the themes of loneliness or separation.

"True story" gang films (*jitsuroku eiga*):
Gang films, often based on true stories, attempting to depict the brutal, eat-or-be-eaten realities of gang life. The genre was pioneered by Kinji Fukasaku and made popular with his 1973 hit *Battles Without Honour and Humanity* (*Jingi naki Tatakai*).

Ninkyo films:
Gangster films set in the period roughly from the beginning of the Meiji era, in 1868, to the early years of the Showa era (1926-1989). They celebrate the traditional *giri-ninjo* ethos, in which the hero risks his life to honour his felt obligation to a gang and its boss, even though he is often an outsider, free to walk away. Nikkatsu's most prominent example of the genre was the ten-part *Symbol of a Man* (*Otoko no Monsho*, 1963-66) series starring Hideki Takahashi.

Mood action *(mudo akushon)*:
A sub-genre of the mid-1960s that combined elements of action and romantic drama, in a noir-ish setting. The best known example is Toshio Masuda's *Red Handkerchief* (*Akai Handkerchief*, 1964).

Youth films (*seishun eiga*):
Films about adolescent love and friendship, and family relations, usually set in contemporary Japan. Nikkatsu's were among the most popular in the 1950s and 1960s, with Sayuri Yoshinaga being the biggest youth film star.

New Action (*Nyu Akushon*):
A sub-genre that became popular in the late 1960s and early 1970s. Made by a new generation of directors and stars, these films reflected the era's social turmoil, while upping the sex and violence ante.

Index

Page references in **bold** refer exclusively to illustrations, though pages referred to as text entries may also feature illustrations.

Original theatrical poster for Seijun Suzuki's "Youth of the Beast" (Yaju no Seishun, 1963).

No Borders, No Limits

C I N E M A C L A S S I C S C O L L E C T I O N

The Cinema Classics Collection from FAB Press is a series of budget-priced studies of historically important movies, genres, actors and directors.

Cinema Classics Collection Volume 1
Witchcraft Through the Ages

Benjamin Christensen's macabre masterpiece from 1922, **Häxan** ['The Witch'] is the first 'film maudit' [literally a 'cursed film'] and can justifiably be considered the world's first cult movie, the first exploitation film, and the original documentary cinema classic. Using the original Danish source material, Jack Stevenson places **Häxan** within the context of Christensen's wider career, and also within the context of the times, and demonstrates how its influence is still being felt today.

ISBN 978-1-903254-42-4, 128 pages
RRP: UK£6.99, US $11.95

Cinema Classics Collection Volume 3
A Violent Professional

With more than seventy appearances in Italian cult movies to his name – ranging from **Django**, **Violent Naples** and **Death Smiles At Murder** to **City of the Living Dead**, **Salon Kitty** and **Bloody Hands of the Law** – Luciano Rossi gets brutalised more regularly and more spectacularly than any of his contemporaries... and he deals it as furiously as he takes it! Stunningly designed, and printed in full colour throughout, this book is a loving tribute to the great unsung hero of Eurotrash cinema.

ISBN 978-1-903254-48-6, 128 pages
RRP: UK£7.99, US $15.95

www.fabpress.com